# Skill Development, Innovations and Entrepreneurship

# Skill Development, Innovations and Entrepreneurship

**Dr. Mohd. Shoeb**
Assistant Professor, Department of Commerce,
Aligarh Muslim University (AMU), Aligarh,
Uttar Pradesh

New Century Publications
New Delhi, India

NEW CENTURY PUBLICATIONS
4800 / 24, Bharat Ram Road,
Ansari Road, Daryaganj,
New Delhi - 110 002 (India)

Tel.: 011 - 4358 7398, 4101 7798, 2324 7798

Email: info@newcenturypublications.com

**www.newcenturypublications.com**

*Editorial office:*
4832/24, Ansari Road, Daryaganj,
New Delhi – 110 002

Tel.: 011-4356 0919



First Published: **2020**

ISBN: **978-81-7708-511-2**

Published by New Century Publications and printed at Milan Enterprises, New Delhi.

Designs: Patch Creative Unit, New Delhi.

PRINTED IN INDIA

# About the Book

Skill development is important because it enhances productivity at the individual, industry and national levels. In India, skill formation is broadly ensured through general education—considered as a provider of generic skills. Other than general education, skill formation efforts consist of vocational education and training and sector-specific programmes for better employability in industry.

National Policy for Skill Development and Entrepreneurship, 2015 aims to bring the world of education and training closer to the world of work to build a strong India. It provides clarity and coherence on how skill development efforts across the country can be aligned within the existing institutional arrangements. The Policy links skill development to improved employability and productivity.

India had declared 2010-20 as the Decade of Innovation. The Government has stressed the need to enunciate a policy to synergize science, technology and innovation and has also established the National Innovation Council (NInC).

Entrepreneurship is the quality of being an entrepreneur, i.e. one who *undertakes an enterprise*. The term puts emphasis on the risk and effort taken by individuals who own and manage a business.

This book provides a comprehensive account of policies and programmes for skill development, innovations and entrepreneurship in India. It is spread over 16 chapters which have been organized into 3 theme parts.

Part I (chapters 1 to 8) is devoted to policies and programmes for skill development in India.

Part II (chapters 9 to 13) covers promotion of science, technology and innovations.

Part III (chapters 14 to 16) deals with entrepreneurship development.

# Author's Profile

**Dr. Mohd. Shoeb** is currently Assistant Professor in the Department of Commerce, Aligarh Muslim University (AMU), Aligarh, Uttar Pradesh. He received his M.Com. and Ph.D. degrees from AMU in 2006 and 2009 respectively. He has published a number of research papers in reputed academic journals including *International Journal of Research in Computer Application and Management (IJRCM)*.

Dr. Shoeb is a member of the editorial review board of *Amity Journal of Finance*. He has attended and presented papers at various conferences and seminars. His areas of research interest include entrepreneurship development and managerial economics.

# Contents

# Preface

Skill development is important because of its contribution to enhancing productivity at the individual, industry and also national levels because of the complementarities that exist between physical capital and human capital on the one hand and between technology and human capital on the other. Fast changing knowledge economies call for new core competencies among all learners in the society. The term *skills* is used in the literature to refer to a wide range of attributes and to that extent there is no clear definition of a skilled worker. In practical terms, the term used is *marketable skill* which commonly refers to any skill/expertise/ability that has a market value, i.e. which has the potential of being utilised for generating income/employment.

Skill development is needed for more jobs and higher productivity. Creating jobs and increasing productivity are at the top of agenda for policymakers across the world. For developing countries that are seeking to grow in an inclusive way and reduce poverty, the challenge of expanding employment and productivity is a sine qua non.

Skills, and skills development, are an essential component of all efforts in this challenging area. Too many workers are simply unprepared to meet the needs of firms, particularly in more competitive economic environments. Systems to provide training are often plagued by weak governance and poor incentives that make them unreliable or ineffective. Weak incentives and support platforms for innovation and entrepreneurship development can stifle creativity and change.

However, the problem is often more complex. In many countries, education systems are not providing young people with the basic skills (cognitive and behavioural) that make them *trainable.* And serious handicaps are inflicted early in life when children are malnourished or insufficiently stimulated. Moreover, rigid labour markets in many countries reduce mobility and make it difficult for workers to find jobs—and for firms to find the right workers.

The foundations of industrial and agricultural advance lie ultimately in the availability and effective use of human skills. Human skills are a formidable asset since they last not merely during one working life but because they are transmitted for generations. If these assets are used effectively, they may well turn out to be one of the most fruitful results of planning.

Modern technology is changing rapidly and no country can hope to maintain a steady pace of advance unless it keeps abreast of current developments. Techniques in turn affect and are affected by economic and social organisation. Certain forms of economic and social organisation are unsuited to or incapable of absorbing new techniques and utilising them to the best advantage. To some extent techniques must of course be adapted to economic and social organisation, but the latter has also to change in order to accommodate new techniques which need to be applied not merely in one or two isolated lines but in several lines of economic activity.

Innovation requires a financial system which is supportive and inclusive and which provides the necessary risk capital to spur innovations and enterprises. Venture funds are recognized globally as the most suitable form of providing risk capital for the growth of innovative technology and breakthrough ideas.

India is in a unique position to mount a strong initiative for affordable innovations for technologies for social and public good by taking advantages of: (a) low expertise costs, (b) vast talent base and (c) residual idealism in the society. However, engagement of multiple stakeholders and creating public private partnership for promoting people-centric research is a challenge to address national goals with specific targets in a time-bound manner. While technologies for public, strategic, and social goods would require collaborative excellence, competitive excellence models for private good would come from industrial sector, as is the case in most developed countries.

It must be borne in mind that scientific explorations and widening the frontiers of knowledge are important activities of all civilised societies. India has had its own treasure house of traditional sciences. India has produced many giants in a variety of disciplines of science during the 20th century. It must be ensured that creativity and excellence are nurtured amongst the younger generation and India contributes to future discoveries and inventions on a scale that is appropriate for its size and history.

The growth and prosperity of all economies remains highly dependent on entrepreneurial activity. Entrepreneurs are the essence of economic growth as they provide a source of income and employment for themselves, create employment for others, produce new and innovative products or services, and drive greater upstream and downstream value-chain activities. Supportive environments are increasingly essential to successful entrepreneurship and these are evolving across the world.

The face of entrepreneurship is also changing. Across the world, entrepreneurs are increasingly young and/or female due to increasing unemployment. The public and private sector each have an important role to play in creating entrepreneurial ecosystems that, in addition to funding, are essential to promoting entrepreneurial success.

Entrepreneurship has been considered the backbone of economic development. It has been well-established that the level of economic growth of a region, to a large extent, depends on the level of entrepreneurial activities in the region. The myth that entrepreneurs are born, no more holds good. Rather, it is well-recognised now that the entrepreneurs can be created and nurtured through appropriate interventions in the form of entrepreneurship development programmes.

Aligarh
*June 2020*

**Mohd. Shoeb**

# Abbreviations/Acronyms

| | |
|---|---|
| **AICTE** | All India Council for Technical Education |
| **AIE** | Alternative and Innovative Education |
| **AIM** | Atal Innovation Mission |
| **ATIs** | Advanced Training Institutes |
| **BDCs** | Business Development Centres |
| **CBSE** | Central Board of Secondary Education |
| **CCRT** | Centre for Cultural Resources and Training |
| **CSIR** | Council of Scientific and Industrial Research |
| **CSR** | Corporate Social Responsibility |
| **DGR** | Directorate General of Resettlement |
| **DGT** | Directorate General of Training |
| **DICs** | District Industries Centres |
| **DIETs** | District Institutes of Education and Training |
| **DISE** | District Information System for Education |
| **E-Hubs** | Entrepreneurship Hubs |
| **FDI** | Foreign Direct Investment |
| **GER** | Gross Enrolment Ratio |
| **HRMP** | Human Resource Mobility Partnerships |
| **ICAR** | Indian Council of Agriculture Research |
| **IISER** | Indian Institute of Science Education and Research |
| **IIT** | Indian Institute of Technology |
| **IMCs** | Institute Management Committees |
| **INDEST** | Indian National Digital Library for Engineering Sciences and Technology |
| **INFLIBNET** | Information for Library Network |
| **IPERPO** | Intellectual Property Education, Research and Public Outreach |
| **IPRs** | Intellectual Property Rights |
| **MES** | Modular Employable Skills |
| **MOOCs** | Massive Open Online Courses |
| **MoU** | Memorandum of Understanding |
| **MSIs** | Multi Skill Institutes |
| **MSMEs** | Micro, Small and Medium Enterprises |

| | |
|---|---|
| **NAAC** | National Accreditation Assessment Council |
| **NAC** | National Advisory Committee |
| **NAI** | National Archives of India |
| **NBA** | National Board of Accreditation |
| **NBCFDC** | National Backward Classes Finance and Development Corporation |
| **NBE** | National Board of Examinations |
| **NCAER** | National Council for Applied Economic Research |
| **NCERT** | National Council of Educational Research and Training |
| **NCGTC** | National Credit Guarantee Trustee Company |
| **NCTE** | National Council for Teacher Education |
| **NCVT** | National Council for Vocational Training |
| **NERIST** | North Eastern Regional Institute of Science and Technology |
| **NET** | National Education Testing |
| **NIOS** | National Institute of Open Schooling |
| **NISER** | National Institute of Science Education and Research |
| **NITTTRs** | National Institutes of Technical Teachers Training and Research |
| **NLM** | National Literacy Mission |
| **NLSI** | New Linguistic Survey of India |
| **NMDFC** | National Minorities Development and Finance Corporation |
| **NOS** | National Occupational Standards |
| **NPE** | National Policy of Education |
| **NPEGEL** | National Programme for Education of Girls at Elementary Level |
| **NSCFDC** | National Scheduled Caste Finance and Development Corporation |
| **NSDA** | National Skill Development Agency |
| **NSDC** | National Skill Development Corporation |
| **NSDCB** | National Skill Development Co-ordination Board |

| | |
|---|---|
| **NSQC** | National Skills Qualification Committee |
| **NSQF** | National Skills Qualification Framework |
| **NSRD** | National Skills Research Division |
| **NSS** | National Service Scheme |
| **NUEPA** | National University of Educational Planning Administration |
| **NVQ** | National Vocational Qualification |
| **NVs** | *Navodaya Vidyalayas* |
| **OJT** | On-the-Job Training |
| **PIU** | Policy Implementation Unit |
| **PMKVY** | *Pradhan Mantri Kaushal Vikas Yojana* |
| **PPP** | Public-Private-Partnership |
| **PSE** | Pre-school Education |
| **PTR** | Pupil Teacher Ratio |
| **QR Code** | Quick Response Code |
| **RBI** | Reserve Bank of India |
| **RPL** | Recognition of Prior Learning |
| **SCERT** | State Council for Educational Research and Training |
| **SERC** | Science and Engineering Research Council |
| **SETU** | Self-employment Talent Utilisation |
| **SHE** | Scholarships for Higher Education |
| **SIEs** | State Institutes of Education |
| **SJE** | Social Justice and Empowerment |
| **SOS** | State Open Schools |
| **SOUs** | State Open Universities |
| **SSA** | *Sarva Shiksha Abhiyan* |
| **SSCs** | Sector Skills Councils |
| **SSDMs** | State Skill Development Missions |
| **STEP** | Skills Toward Employment and Productivity |
| **SVs** | Skill Vouchers |
| **TEQIP** | Technical Education Quality Improvement Programme |
| **TLC** | Total Literacy Campaigns |
| **TLE** | Teaching Learning Equipment |
| **ToT** | Training of Trainers |

| | |
|---|---|
| **TTIs** | Teacher Training Institutions |
| **TVET** | Technical and Vocational Education and Training |
| **UEE** | Universalization of Elementary Education |
| **UEN** | Unique Enterprise Number |
| **UGC** | University Grants Commission |
| **VE** | Vocational Education |
| **VECs** | Village Education Committees |
| **VET** | Vocational Education and Training |
| **WCD** | Women and Child Development |
| **WOB** | Women-owned Business |

# Part I
## Skill Development Policy and Initiatives

# 1

# Skill Development: An Introduction

Occupational patterns are changing; and new jobs and job titles, job enlargement, job enrichment, and new flexible work arrangements are emerging. Employment demands are shifting towards higher skill categories. It is imperative, therefore, for India to move up the skill-ladder and produce a larger number of people with higher education and generic training for new types of knowledge work, both in high skill services and high technology industrial production. Knowledge professionals will need support from middle-skilled workers in new knowledge and technology areas. The skill development system will need to meet this challenge. The response time is limited as the rate of change is high and accelerating.

## 1.1 Meaning and Importance of Skill Development

The term *skills* is used in the literature to refer to a wide range of attributes and to that extent there is no clear definition of a skilled worker. In practical terms, the term used is *marketable skill* which commonly refers to any skill/expertise/ability that has a market value, i.e. which has the potential of being utilised for generating income/employment.

Skill development is important because of its contribution to enhancing productivity at the individual, industry and also national levels because of the complementarities that exist between physical capital and human capital on the one hand and between technology and human capital on the other. Fast changing knowledge economies call for new core competencies among all learners in the society.

The level of technology and the concomitant levels of skills directly determine productivity of labour. Improvement of skill enhances labour productivity even with the existing technology.

Labour productivity determines the potential relative shares of both labour and capital. Rise in labour productivity is a necessary condition for raising living standards of both wage and non-wage earners. Potential for better wages of workers and remuneration of the self-employed and the living standards of the working poor increase *parri passu* with increased productivity of labour. Moreover, higher incomes and wages of the working poor would contribute to increased aggregate effective demand for goods and services produced both in informal and formal sectors stimulating investment and growth in both the sectors. Thus, a multiplier effect may result leading to faster growth all across.

Making the most effective use of workers—using all of them, and using them to their greatest productivity—is vital. And while insufficient demand for workers remains a problem in many parts of the developing world, persistently high unemployment rates are partly a function of skills mismatches, the result of workers inadequately equipped for the demands of employers. This is sometimes because of insufficient education, but also because education and training did not provide the skills that employers want. Low returns to work effort—from some forms of self-employment as well as wage work—may be due to inadequate demand for high-productivity work or insufficient complementary factors such as technology and infrastructure. However, low skill levels associated with low-income work are also responsible.

As countries become richer and move up the value-added chain, the skills demanded will change. Bottlenecks will become more evident, constraining growth. Increasingly, labour productivity will depend on high-level cognitive skills (such as analysis, problem solving, and communication) and behavioural skills (such as discipline and work effort). These higher productivity skills are what employers now demand. Evidence shows that, as economies develop, the demand for interactive and analytical skills in the workplace increases steeply and continually, while that for manual and routine cognitive skills falls. There is also evidence that as middle-income countries become richer, more employers consider skills an important constraint on business development.

In many economies, employers are searching for workers who possess behavioural skills such as teamwork, diligence, creativity, and entrepreneurship, essential to thrive in today's rapidly evolving, technologically driven globalized economies. Thus, just improving workers' technical and vocational skills will not always meet employers' needs—systems that build skills will also have to ensure that these added behavioural attributes are in place.

The efficacy of training later in life is heavily influenced by workers' early years. Behavioural skills needed for higher productivity jobs, built through learning from families and schools, are difficult to impart later in life. The ability to acquire higher cognitive skills such as creativity and entrepreneurship critically depends on the amount and quality of stimulation and education received in childhood. As a result, workers who have poor early childhood environments or inadequate or insufficient basic education will be less able to flexibly acquire the higher level skills employers need and are less likely to be employable or fully productive.

In short, skills are at the core of improving employment outcomes of individuals and increasing productivity and growth of countries. This is particularly relevant as today's developing and emerging countries seek higher sustained growth rates. Most of them face serious demographic challenges, including "youth bulge" of new jobseekers.

## 1.2 Requirements of a Sound Skills Building Strategy

Skill development is needed for more jobs and higher productivity. Creating jobs and increasing productivity are at the top of agenda for policymakers across the world. For developing countries that are seeking to grow in an inclusive way and reduce poverty, the challenge of expanding employment and productivity is a sine qua non.

Skills, and skills development, are an essential component

of all efforts in this challenging area. Too many workers are simply unprepared to meet the needs of firms, particularly in more competitive economic environments. Systems to provide training are often plagued by weak governance and poor incentives that make them unreliable or ineffective. Weak incentives and support platforms for innovation and entrepreneurship development can stifle creativity and change.

However, the problem is often more complex. In many countries, education systems are not providing young people with the basic skills (cognitive and behavioural) that make them *trainable.* And serious handicaps are inflicted early in life when children are malnourished or insufficiently stimulated. Moreover, rigid labour markets in many countries reduce mobility and make it difficult for workers to find jobs—and for firms to find the right workers.

In this context, it is indispensable to have the following comprehensive and adaptive systems to build skills.

1. Right start for children.
2. Ensuring that all students learn.
3. Job-relevant skills.
4. Entrepreneurship and innovation.
5. Matching supply of skills with demand.
6. Technological upgradation.

### 1.3 Right Start for Children

This can be done by developing the technical, cognitive, and behavioural skills conducive to high productivity and flexibility in the work environment through early child development (ECD), emphasizing nutrition, stimulation, and basic cognitive skills. Handicaps built early in life are difficult if not impossible to remedy later in life and that effective ECD programs can have a very high payoff. Failing to invest in ECD is costly, if not impossible, to compensate for later in life. The skills developed in early childhood—from birth to primary school entry—form the basis of future learning and labour market success. Early childhood development (ECD) enhances a child's ability to learn, to work with others, to be patient, and to develop a wide range of other foundational skills for formal learning and interactions in the school years and beyond.

A failure to develop these skills can lead to long-term and often irreversible effects on education, health, and productive earnings, imposing significant costs for both individuals and societies. Inadequate nutrition between conception and age 2 leads to serious cognitive delays among school-age children. And linguistic and cognitive delays can accumulate rapidly if not addressed. The window of opportunity is small because these foundational skills are best formed in the early years. Failing to invest in them is costly to compensate for later in life, if not impossible.

Defining ECD concepts and interventions ECD programmes enhance the physical, cognitive, socio-emotional, and linguistic development of children from conception to primary school entry. Optimal investments in each area of ECD are required at each age:

1. Ensuring the health and nutrition of the pregnant and lactating mother can ensure good physical development of the fetus and good breast milk. This is most important from conception to the first 6 months of life. Interventions include prenatal care, vitamin supplements, and counselling mothers in nutrition and breastfeeding.
2. Immunizations and regular health checkups should start at birth and continue through age 6.
3. Breastfeeding for very young infants is desired because of its nutritional and protective benefits. Depending on the context, the longer the breastfeeding, the better for the infant, though solid foods are expected to be introduced by the age of 6 months.
4. With cognitive stimulation by caregivers or teachers, a child benefits from exposure to shapes, numbers, and formal ideas starting at age 3.
5. For linguistic stimulation, caregivers should talk to, read to, sing to, and verbally interact with children starting at birth.

6. Healthy emotional development begins at birth through the presence of and communication to the child of a caring environment long before he or she can express such emotions. Such practices include holding and touching the child, making eye contact, and communicating a safe environment.
7. By age 3, children learn to interact and negotiate with their peers. If these skills are not learned in early childhood, they are difficult to learn later in life.

Delivering the whole package is most efficient since each domain supports the successful development of other domains. By age 6, the well-developed child should be physically, cognitively, and socio-emotionally ready to enter primary school. Any areas of deficiency are difficult, if not impossible, to remedy later in life. ECD services can be delivered through various channels, largely dependent on the dimension of the package and the context. The most common channels are as under:

1. **Centre-based:** Preschools are perhaps the best understood delivery mechanism. Those focused on child development work with children and their parents on all domains of ECD. Since centres offer peer interactions that are less available in the home, it is strongly recommended that children aged 3-6 participate in preschools.
2. **Public Health Centres:** While these centres often focus on physical development, they also measure development in other domains and counsel caregivers on linguistic and socio-emotional stimulation and overall care.
3. **Counselling:** This service may be centre-based or provided in the home. The social worker provides classes for parents, usually mothers, on the proper feeding of children, the importance and process for immunizations, the provision of socio-emotional stimulation, and cognitive development. This training can begin before the child is born.
4. **Peer-to-Peer Learning:** Also a form of counselling, this intervention provides training to community members who

share information about the various forms of care with community groups.

5. **Media Campaigns:** Through radio, television, and posters, information about proper care and stimulation of children can be shared with a broad and dispersed population.

These types of interventions may be offered by the public or private sectors, be publicly or privately funded, and be implemented by any social ministry.

Strong evidence from around the world shows the impact of ECD throughout the lifetime. Children who participate in quality ECD programs have higher cognitive development and overall school readiness on primary school entry, lower repetition and dropout rates in the early grades, greater learning in school, and higher school completion rates.

ECD interventions are among the most cost-effective investments a country can make in its people. So, ECD investments should be a top priority for efforts to promote employment and productivity later in life in many countries—and for the poorest and most disadvantaged groups in all countries.

## 1.4 Ensuring that All Students Learn

Schools are expected to teach basic competencies that enable students to acquire the skills that would help them make informed life choices and that would later be valued by employers and useful for self-employment. In fact, the seeds of these competencies should have been planted from infancy, and schools should develop them. These competencies include the following:

1. Problem-solving skills.
2. Learning skills.
3. Communication skills.
4. Personal skills.
5. Social skills.

In addition to these basic competencies, skills that are more directly required for work can be developed through schooling:

1. Cognitive skills as demonstrated by an intellectual grasp of the subject matter of various academic subjects such as language, mathematics, various pure and applied sciences, and the social sciences.
2. Psychomotor skills for the tasks to be performed in an occupation, job or business (operating a lathe or a weaving loom, preparing architectural plans, installing equipment) and the ability to apply the skills in practice.
3. Affective skills relating to a person's attitudes toward timeliness, accuracy, and general commitment to quality and performance, and perception of the meaning and value of work, concept of self and others.

The lists illustrate the multiple dimensions of job-relevant skills that go beyond simple book learning and the ability to execute a specific task. But information on learning outcomes indicates that schools in many developing countries are failing to teach foundational cognitive skills, much less the "expert thinking and complex communication" and occupational skills needed to function effectively in the modern labour market.

With so many students not learning, higher enrolment rates will not necessarily translate into productivity gains for workers or economic growth. This is a huge opportunity lost. Education remains one of the most powerful instruments for improving lives, reducing poverty and ultimately laying the foundation for economic growth.

Developing countries have made great progress in expanding supply and ensuring access to schools, including for disadvantaged children. In addition, they have used interventions, such as the abolition of school fees and scholarships, cash transfers to compensate for the opportunity cost of school attendance, and vouchers that give poor students the choice to use privately provided services, that can strengthen demand for education, thus raising enrolments and reducing schooling inequalities.

Together, these measures account for notable increases in enrolment rates at the primary and secondary education levels.

Now countries need to ensure that "schooled" youth leave school with useful, robust skills. Whether from inadequate or misused educational investment, poor teaching, or ineffective systems, poor learning wastes both public and private resources. It leads to higher repetition, failure and dropout rates, and lower completion and transition rates. Ultimately, poor learning outcomes also limit a country's potential for economic growth.

What policies improve learning? Traditional policies and programs that focus on inputs regardless of outcomes are likely to be wasteful and ineffective. In contrast, those that measure results, address systemic issues and support a long-term vision are likely to succeed. The building blocks of an education system are learning standards, good teachers, adequate resources, and a proper regulatory environment. But to enhance system performance, these building blocks should be connected through an integrated system of incentives, rewards, and sanctions.

1. **Standards:** By defining clearly the knowledge and skills that students are expected to gain, they will better understand what is expected of them, schools will cater their programs accordingly, teachers will know what they will be held accountable for, and school managers will be challenged to seek the means to raise the level of teaching and learning.
2. **Teachers:** Most teacher-related investments focus on pre- and in-service training, but to improve the teaching force, policies must not only establish and enforce proper qualifications (through training and support services) but also provide teachers the incentives for good performance.
3. **Resources:** Without adequate resources for key inputs, it is hard to achieve the standards and goals set for a school system. But also as important as spending levels are the proper allocation of resources to different uses, equitable distribution across schools, and management that minimizes waste and leakage.
4. **Regulatory Environment:** Managing the various inputs requires monitoring and control to ensure adequate provision.

This demands a regulatory environment that encourages good governance, has clear criteria for establishing schools, establishes mechanisms that allow for choice and voice, and promotes equity in financing and results.

Schools can provide some measure of protection by teaching students about hygiene, good eating habits, the dangers of substance abuse, and safe sex. Schools are also a ready-made centre for delivering child and adolescent nutrition and health services.

Lessons from research and ground experience indicate that the key decisions about education systems can be grouped into three: how much autonomy to allow and to whom, accountability from whom and for what, and how to assess performance.

1. **Autonomy:** Students and teachers perform best in a climate of high expectations supported by strong teacher-student relations so that students and their teachers are ready to invest effort. Greater autonomy can give schools the flexibility to empower teachers and parents, thus improving teacher morale. In countries that perform well, local authorities and schools have substantial responsibility for educational content and resource use. But efforts to move more decision-making to the local level need support from the centre in matters of evaluation and assistance for weaker schools.
2. **Accountability:** To improve learning, school autonomy must be accompanied by an accountability framework that enhances community and parental interest. Accountability contributes to quality by involving the stakeholders and by setting clear goals and standards for the system. If schools and students are responsible for results, they will ensure that homework is done, that students and teachers are in class, that pedagogy is appropriate, and that administrators acquire the appropriate school inputs.
3. **Assessment:** If greater autonomy and accountability are to lead to policies for quality, measures of learning outcomes are essential. High-performing countries use information to constantly focus on improvements over time. To assess

system performance, countries usually rely on national standardized tests, and for cross-country comparisons, on regional or international achievement tests—although many developing countries still do not use these instruments to assess them school system. Such tests complement the easier-to-measure enrolment, repetition, dropout, and completion rates. But measurement is only half the battle. Countries should also strengthen their capacity to analyze and understand results, engage in policy debate using those results, and feed the results back as information into policymaking.

There is no magic bullet for achieving system-wide success, but several countries have achieved significant gains by using student assessments, implementing curricular change, and giving schools more autonomy.

Lower-income countries with lower enrolment rates and achievement levels have also made progress by focusing on their goals for both enrolments and learning. They have adopted national and international benchmarking as a way to monitor results. For example, in India the school report cards developed by the District Information System for Education summarize school information in an easy to read format, allowing parents and stakeholders access to information not previously available to hold schools and authorities to account. The data from the report cards are available on the web, a potentially powerful tool for local accountability.

If effective, schools lay the foundational skills for youth to be productive and creative workers, securing for them opportunities to live well and contribute to their communities. These skills are broader than those that are currently being measured in developing countries because they include also teamwork, communication, and the ability to innovate and solve problems. But countries' efforts today to measure reading comprehension levels, arithmetic acumen, and science understanding are a step in the right direction.

# 2

# Job-relevant Skills

Market failures in skill formation are common, and many governments intervene to minimize the risk of under-investments in training. The instruments typically involve the governance of training provision, the public financing of training, and the way information about training services and their outcomes is generated and packaged to inform trainees, employers, and other key stakeholders. These aspects of policy design influence the incentives of individuals and firms to invest in skills and shape those of training providers to deliver effective and responsive services.

There are basically two junctures when the training occurs: before employment and on-the-job. The training includes instruction in classrooms, laboratories, workshops, apprenticeship arrangements, and internships. Country conditions and the occupation influence the choice of these options, but the contribution of both pre-employment and on-the-job training can be improved to promote job-relevant skills and align them more closely to demand signals from the labour market.

## 2.1 What are Job-relevant Skills?

Job-relevant skills refer to a set of competencies valued by employers and useful for self-employment. They include skills relevant to the specific job of the worker as well as other skills that enhance his or her productivity. These other skills include the following:

1. Problem-solving skills or the capacity to think critically and analyze.
2. Learning skills or the ability to acquire new knowledge ("learning to learn"), distil lessons from experience, and apply them in search of innovations.

3. Communication skills, including reading and writing, collecting and using information to communicate with others, and using a foreign language and information and communication technologies (ICTs) as communication tools.
4. Personal skills for self-management, making sound judgments, and managing risks.
5. Social skills to collaborate with and motivate others in a team, manage client relations, exercise leadership, resolve conflicts, and develop social networks.

Because country conditions differ, there is no ideal reform package to balance the supply of skills imparted through pre-employment training programs and the employer demand for skills. The challenge is creating the environment for providers of training to have the incentives to respond to the needs of the labour market.

### 2.2 Pre-employment Skills Development

Perhaps the most frequent complaint, especially about public institutions that offer TVET, is that the system produces the same graduates year after year with little regard to labour market signals. In addition, costs are high, public support is weak for what is considered a poor route to jobs, and the curriculum is often narrowly geared toward jobs in the formal sector, which in most low-income countries is tiny and not growing fast enough to offer many new jobs.

### 2.3 On-the-job Training (OJT)

OJT contributes much to the stock of human capital, with estimates ranging from a quarter to half of all human capital formation in the United States. It tends to favour workers with higher levels of educational attainment and occurs more frequently in larger firms and in more dynamic, export-oriented sectors. The bias often puts countries in a paradox, with firms complaining about skill shortages while also being unwilling or unable to upgrade their own workers' skills through OJT.

Technical and vocational education and training (TVET) programmes are highly diverse in the competencies they impart. Their entry requirements also vary greatly, from the fairly modest (courses on simple welding jobs), to the moderately demanding (courses for tool and die makers, aerospace-certified welders, air traffic controllers, high voltage technicians), to the highly demanding (courses for engineers, designers, scientists, neurosurgeons).

The diversity implies that training occurs in a correspondingly wide variety of settings: in schools that offer TVET courses and in post-secondary institutions such as community colleges, polytechnics, universities and other specialized institutes (and indeed in overseas institutions in esoteric fields). The courses offered at universities are generally viewed as professional training rather than TVET; the training of teachers (and sometimes that of health workers, including doctors) is treated likewise. The term TVET is thus often used tacitly to refer to the training of other workers, with vocational training typically assumed to be geared to trainees expecting jobs as skilled workers at the lower to mid-level, and technical training mostly directed at those aiming for skilled jobs at higher levels of responsibility.

Smaller firms in most countries are reluctant to provide training on the job, for fear of losing trained workers to other firms and for lack of access to credit and information about training. An unfavourable business environment acts as a further impediment by weakening firm incentives to compete, innovate, and train workers. But even under more favourable environments, firms and workers may still under-invest in skills. In such cases, financial incentives can foster OJT. In low-income settings or for the informal sector, traditional apprenticeships can be an option.

For most large and well-established firms, OJT is often so productive that they invest in it with little government intervention. Examples of such initiatives can be found in India's leading companies. Infosys, a software technology giant, completed a new 300-faculty Global Education Centre in 2009 with a training capacity of 14,000 seats, dedicated to enhancing the competency of its staff.

### 2.4 Skills Certification Systems

One important aspect of a strategy to facilitate and promote the acquisition of job-relevant skills involves a framework for workers and firms to have clear information on those skills and on acceptable standards. Skills certification has become important to employers as a quality assurance mechanism that recognizes and certifies an individual's skills and competencies.

Skills certification is often referred to as competency-based certification. As modes and pathways of learning become more diverse, skills certification fulfils many objectives.

First, it recognizes skills and competencies regardless of the way in which they were acquired or of the job-seekers' educational background.

Second, it allows employers to compare individuals' skills across the labour market.

Third, it is a way to match the skills acquired through training or other means with the skills required to perform a job.

Fourth, its less immediate objectives are to increase occupational mobility, promote lifelong learning, and enable international and intergenerational comparative analysis. Often, skills certification can be organized in a national qualification framework, which defines a single set of criteria for specified levels of learning and thus increases transparency and eases recognition of qualifications by labour market participants.

### 2.5 Matching Supply of Skills with Demand

Even if individuals have the "right" skills to be productive and creative, employment and productivity can be hampered if labour markets do not function well. Employers need the flexibility to manage their human resources. Workers need to move freely between jobs and regions. And employers have to find the skills they need, and workers the jobs that put their skills to best use. When workers cannot move freely, both output and productivity growth are reduced.

Youths entering the labour market for the first time, and thus lacking work experience and professional references, are likely to face more difficulties signalling their skills to potential employers. This problem can be amplified when there is no proper certification or accreditation for different training centres or universities. Indeed, there is some evidence that the transition to stable formal jobs involves a period where young workers alternate between short-term/low productivity jobs in the informal sector. The problem is likely to be even more severe for informal sector workers lacking university or training diplomas.

Governments can facilitate labour mobility and job searches through various interventions, including a better combination of job and income protection policies and more proactive approaches to employment services and skills certification. The other side of the coin in efforts to enhance labour mobility involves expanding coverage of social protection systems to protect workers' incomes in the face of job loss. In many cases, innovations in income protection systems can provide an alternative to expensive severance pay systems—thus better protecting workers while facilitating mobility.

In fact, employment services are being revamped in several middle-income countries. International experience shows what's important for the successful design of these programmes:

1. Providing incentives for job-seekers and employers to join.
2. Integrating employment services with training and competency assessment programs.
3. Decentralizing management and expanding the role of the private sector with clear targets.
4. Exploiting information technologies.

Skills are at the core of improving individuals' employment outcomes and increasing countries' productivity and growth. This is particularly relevant as today's developing and emerging countries seek higher sustained growth rates. Most of them face serious demographic challenges—from a *youth bulge* of new job-seekers in Africa and the Middle East, to a demographic transition of shrinking labour forces in Eastern Europe and Central and East Asia. As countries become richer and move up the value-added chain, the skills demanded will change. Bottlenecks will become more evident, constraining growth. Increasingly, labour productivity will depend on high-level cognitive skills (such as analysis, problem solving, and communication) and behavioural skills (such as discipline and work effort).

These higher productivity skills are what employers now demand. A simple conceptual framework—skills toward employment and productivity (STEP)—can help policymakers, analysts, and researchers think through the design of systems to impart skills that enhance productivity and growth. Pulling together what is known about the elements of a successful skills development strategy, it can guide the preparation of diagnostic work on skills, and subsequently the design of policies across sectors to create productive employment and promote economic growth.

The skill development initiatives harness inclusivity and reduce divisions such as male/female, rural/urban, organized/unorganized employment and traditional and contemporary workplaces. The skill development initiatives support the supply of trained workers who are adjustable dynamically to the changing demands of employment and technologies. This policy promotes excellence and meets the requirements of knowledge economy.

Skill development initiatives should not discriminate between private or public delivery and place importance on outcomes, users' choice and competition among training providers and their accountability. Skill development initiatives support employment generation, economic growth and social development processes. Skill development policy is an integral part of comprehensive economic, labour and social policies and programmes. A framework for better coordination among various Ministries, States, industry and other stakeholders should be established.

**2.6 Globalisation and Skill Development**

Globalisation implies widening and deepening integration with the *globe*, i.e. with people and processes abroad. The trend towards the evolution of a global society is generally thought of in economic terms and in terms of the consequences of the revolution in communication technologies. There is undoubtedly much greater economic integration among the nations of the world today. Globalisation is widely seen as the most important factor that could influence economies of nations the world over in the new millennium. The rapid advancement in information technology and communications has made it not just possible but absolutely essential for economies of the world to adapt or fall by the wayside.

The 1990s witnessed a paradigm shift towards market-oriented economic policies and a careful dismantling of obstacles in its wake. This has helped the smaller, emerging economies gain access to world markets, emergent technologies and collaborations. This has also given them a window to the developed world and helped them understand the significant role of globalisation as an instrument, which could be utilised not just to achieve economic efficiency, but also eradicate poverty.

Globalisation has also resulted in the creation of a new business framework. More changes can be expected in the business scenario specifically in terms of openness, adaptiveness and responsiveness. The most important dimensions of economic globalisation are: (a) breaking down of national barriers, (b) international spread of trade, financial and production activities and (c) growing power of transnational corporations and international financial institutions in these processes. While economic globalisation is a very uneven process, with increased trade and investment being focused in a few countries, almost all countries are greatly affected by this process.

A major feature of globalisation is the growing concentration and monopolisation of economic resources and power by transnational corporations and by global financial firms and funds. This process has been termed transnationalisation, in which fewer and fewer transnational corporations are gaining a large and rapidly increasing proportion of world economic resources, production and market shares. Where a multinational company used to dominate the market of a single product, a big transnational company (TNC) now typically produces or trades in an increasing multitude of products, services and sectors. Through mergers and acquisitions, fewer and fewer of these TNCs now control a larger and larger share of the global market, whether in commodities, manufactures or services.

Another feature of the current globalisation process is the globalisation of national policies and policy-making mechanism. National policies (including economic, social, cultural and technological) that until recently were determined by the States and people within a country have increasingly come under the influence of international agencies and processes or by big private corporations and financial players. This has led to the narrowed ability of governments and people to make choices from options in economic, social and cultural policies.

Most developing countries have seen their independent policy-making mechanism capacity eroded, and have to adopt policies influenced by other entities, which may on balance be detrimental to the countries concerned. The developed countries, where the major economic players reside, and which also control the processes and policies of international economic agencies, are better able to maintain control over their own national policies as well as determine the policies and practices of international institutions and the global system. However, it is also true that the large corporations have taken over a large part of decision-making even in the developed countries, at the expense of the power of the state or political and social leaders.

To promote excellence, a significant number of well-performing institutions should be assisted to develop into institutions of excellence. These institutions should be generously resourced, equipped with internationally comparable facilities and high quality faculty. These institutions should be networked with a number of training institutions in their vicinity and serve as lead institutions in supporting their development.

To sum up, for Indian economy, skill development poses major challenges and also opens up unprecedented doors of opportunity. The magnitude of the skill development challenge can be estimated by the fact that only 3 percent of the existing workforce of India can be called skilled. In an increasingly connected world, where national frontiers are yielding to cross-border outsourcing, it is not inconceivable that in the near future India can become a global reservoir of skilled person power.

The principal problems of poor literacy and numeracy often prevent informal sector workers from participating successfully in the conventional training programmes, even if they perceive the need for training. Training can also be prohibitive in terms of costs, both direct and indirect. Even token fees for the training can form a real barrier for participation in training. Working hours are often long and any time off from the productive work means loss of income, which most cannot afford. This would affect the willingness of workers to join a training programme, even if it is relevant and easily accessible.

Strengthening the educational system and universalizing access to it is thus an essential prerequisite for widespread skill development, particularly when the skill mix needs to change to accommodate the needs of greater integration with the knowledge economy.

# 3

# Stakeholders and Initial Efforts for Skill Development in India

Presently, India is one of the youngest nations in the world with more than 62 percent of its population in the working age group (15-59 years), and more than 54 percent of its total population below 25 years of age. Its population pyramid is expected to bulge across the 15-59 age group over the next decade. It is further estimated that the average age of the population in India by 2020 will be 29 years as against 40 years in USA, 46 years in Europe and 47 years in Japan.

In fact, during the next 20 years the labour force in the industrialized world is expected to decline by 4 percent, while in India it will increase by 32 percent. This poses a formidable challenge and a huge opportunity. To reap this demographic dividend which is expected to last for next 25 years, India needs to equip its workforce with employable skills and knowledge so that they can contribute substantively to the economic growth of the country.

Skill development is critical for achieving faster, sustainable and inclusive growth on the one hand and for providing decent employment opportunities to the growing young population on the other. The demographic window of opportunity available to India would make India the skill capital of world. India would be in position to meet the requirement of technically trained manpower not only for its growing economy but also of the aging advanced economies of the world...However, skilling this large and growing young population from an exceedingly small base would be a big challenge for India.

## 3.1 Objectives of Skill Development

Skills and knowledge are the driving forces of economic

growth and social development for any country. Countries with higher and better levels of skills adjust more effectively to the challenges and opportunities of world of work. Potentially, the target group for skill development comprises all those in the labour force, including those entering the labour market for the first time.

The objectives of skill development in India can be construed as under:

1. Rapid and inclusive growth.
2. Enhancing employability and ability of individuals to adapt to changing technologies and labour market demands.
3. Improving productivity and living standards of the people.
4. Strengthening competitiveness of the country.
5. Attracting investment in skill development.
6. Creating opportunities for all to acquire skills throughout life, and especially for youth, women and disadvantaged groups.
7. Promoting commitment by all stakeholders to own skill development initiatives.
8. Developing a high-quality skilled workforce relevant to current and emerging employment market needs.
9. Enabling the establishment of flexible delivery mechanisms that respond to the characteristics of a wide range of needs of stakeholders.
10. Enable effective coordination between different ministries, the Centre and the States and public and private providers.

## 3.2 Role and Responsibilities of Stakeholders

### 3.2.1 Role and Responsibilities of Central and State Governments:

1. Setting up priority and policy planning-statistics gathering.
2. Providing regulatory framework and enabling environment for stakeholders.
3. Devising financing mechanism, reward and promotional framework.
4. Capacity building of social partners.
5. Monitoring, evaluation and dissemination of information.

6. Facilitating international co-operation.
7. Setting up of a qualification framework and quality assurance mechanism.
8. Preparation of work plans to meet sector-specific skill sets.

**3.2.2 Role and Responsibilities of Employers:**

1. Owning skill development activities.
2. Identification of competencies and setting up of competency standards.
3. Skill demand analysis and curriculum development.
4. Facilitating training of trainers.
5. Delivery of training, monitoring and evaluation.
6. Participation in examination and certification.
7. Participation in affiliation and accreditation process.
8. Sharing of work place experience, machinery and equipment.
9. Support by way of physical, financial and human resources.
10. Facilitating employment of trained graduates.
11. Supporting skill development initiatives of other public and private agencies.
12. Implementing apprenticeship schemes.
13. Investing in skill development activities.

**3.2.3 Role and Responsibilities of Trade Unions:**

1. Assisting in developing competency standards.
2. Assisting in course designing, examination and certification.
3. Raising awareness about the benefit of training, skill development plans and activities among the workers.
4. Promoting skill upgradation and lifelong learning among the workers.
5. Running special skill development institutes for skill development of workers.
6. Promoting investment in skill development among the employers.

**3.2.4 Role and Responsibilities of Civil Society Bodies:**

1. Raising awareness about skill development plans and activities among the public.
2. Implementing skill development programmes of the government.

3. Assisting in developing competency standards.
4. Assisting in course designing, examination and certification.
5. Promoting lifelong learning among the public.
6. Promoting dignity of labour among the public.
7. Sharing experience of learning with others.

## 3.3 System of Skill Development in India

In India, skill formation is broadly through general education as a provider of generic skills. Vocational education and training provide marketable industry specific skills for better employability. Other than general education, skill formation efforts consist of the following: (a) vocational education, (b) vocational training and (c) sector-specific programmes to address the issues of skill formation and enhancement.

Within vocational training, distinction can be made between the formal and the informal streams both of which take place under the aegis of the government as well as the private and non-government agencies. Broadly, the following four systems cater to the training needs: (a) the governmental formal training system, (b) the governmental system that focuses exclusively on the informal sector, (c) non-governmental (private as well as NGO) network of formal training institutions and (d) the non-governmental (mostly NGO-led) principally non-formal training programmes for the informal sector.

Skill development programmes are undertaken by various ministries and departments, commissions, councils, autonomous bodies and institutions as well as public-private partnership bodies. Ministry of Skill Development and Entrepreneurship (MSDE), Ministry of Human Resources Development, and Ministry of Labour and Employment are the three major ministries responsible for skill development. [1] Most of the initiatives by other ministries/departments are sectoral in nature and target group oriented.

Most of these schemes and programmes are administered at the field level by the departments and agencies of the respective State Governments or other non-government organisations identified for the purpose. The funds flow downwards and the State Governments are usually assigned the task of implementing as well as monitoring the skill formation programmes on a routine basis. Alternatively, the Central Government departments entrust a number of their programmes directly to non-government organisations. This sometimes results in overlapping of efforts in the implementation of the programmes.

**3.3.1 Private Sector Initiatives for Skill Building:** Private sector initiatives can be broadly categorised into the following four types: (a) where private entrepreneurs or corporations establish training centres/institutes on a for-profit basis, (b) where private corporations impart training to people who get absorbed as skilled workforce in their own units, (c) where they enter into partnerships with public agencies and become the vehicles for training delivery and sometimes finance and (d) where corporate houses set up public trusts or foundations with a development agenda to build the capacities of local communities to be self-reliant and create systems that utilize human and physical capital in a sustainable manner as an integral part of their corporate social responsibility (CSR) mandate.

Private sector initiatives in skill building tend to be more linked to industry demand and hence avoid the wastages associated with supply-led initiatives. However, these are likely to be forthcoming only in response to existing demand and where skilling is likely to have a direct link with profitability. For a large segment of workers in the informal sector, these considerations are not enough and their skilling needs go far beyond those that are likely to be addressed directly by the private sector.

**3.3.2 Initiatives of NGOs in Skill Building:** NGOs interventions range from offering formal ITI courses [approved by National Council for Vocational Training

(NCVT)] to a wide range of non-formal courses. Typically, NGOs devise their own curricula, provide their own training and have their own certification procedures. Very often, they have contacts with employers in the neighbouring areas which provide placements for the trainees. It is often also reported that placement in jobs for those trained are high and that trained workers earn higher wages. There are two types of approaches being followed: (a) training only on basic or upgraded skills and then leave the trainees to seek wage employment or start their own enterprises and (b) a *holistic* package of skill development, basic entrepreneurship training and assistance in availing credit facilities etc. Some NGOs even *handhold* the trainees for a certain period.

Thus, the non-government initiatives, whether by the private sector or by NGOs, address some of the deficiencies that exist in existing government-led systems. They provide training that is demand-led with signals being provided by the market. NGOs adopt a more integrated approach, with different emphasis across different kinds of organisations, but their interventions are too small and dispersed to make a significant difference in terms of the number of workers trained. Further, they suffer from the problems of inconsistent curriculum, lack of certification and standardisation.

### 3.4 Skill Development Initiative (SDI), 2007

The Ministry of Labour and Employment launched SDI in 2007 as a five year project. During this period, 1 million persons were trained or their existing skills tested and certified under modular employable skills (MES) framework.

The objectives of the scheme were the following:

1. To provide vocational training to school leavers, existing workers, ITI graduates etc. to improve their employability by optimally utilizing the infrastructure available in government, private institutions and the industry. Existing skills of the persons were also tested and certified under this scheme.

2. To build capacity in the area of development of competency standards, course curricula, learning material and assessment standards in the country. The minimum age limit for persons to take part in the scheme was 14 years but there was no upper age limit.

The key features of the scheme were the following:

1. Demand driven short-term training courses based on modular employable skills (MES) decided in consultation with the industry.
2. Central Government facilitated and promoted training while industry, private sector and State Governments trained the persons.
3. Optimum utilization of the existing infrastructure was made to make training cost effective.
4. Flexible delivery mechanism (part-time, weekends, full-time, onsite/offsite) was adopted to suit the needs of various target groups.
5. Different levels of programmes were introduced (foundation level as well as skill up-gradation) to meet the demands of various target groups.
6. Services of existing or retired faculty or guest faculty were utilized.
7. Courses were available for persons having completed 5th standard.
8. Testing and certification of skills acquired informally.
9. Testing of skills of trainees by independent assessing bodies, which were not involved in training delivery, to ensure that it was done impartially.
10. Essence of the scheme was in the certification that would be nationally and internationally recognized.

## 3.5 Co-ordinated Action on Skill Development

Skill building can be viewed as an instrument to improve the effectiveness and contribution of labour to the overall production. It is as an important ingredient to push the production possibility frontier outward and to take growth rate of the economy to a higher trajectory. Skill building could also be seen as an instrument to empower the individual and improve his/her social acceptance or value.

Coordinated action on skill development as proposed by Planning Commission was approved by the Cabinet on May 15, 2008. The coordinated action was the major initiative for achieving inclusive growth and development through coordination and harmonization of skill development initiatives of different players. The action aimed at creation of a pool of skilled manpower with adequate skills that meet the employment requirements across various sectors of the national economy. The approved Coordinated Action on Skill Development envisaged setting up of a three-tier institutional structure involving Prime Minister's National Council on Skill Development (NCSD) for policy direction to be supported by National Skill Development Coordination Board (NSDCB) and National Skill Development Corporation (NSDC). The institutional structure was put in place in 2008 itself.

**3.5.1 Prime Minister's National Council on Skill Development (NCSD):** In pursuance of the decision of the Cabinet at its meeting held on May 15, 2008 on Coordinated Action for Skill Development and setting up of the National Skill Development Corporation, Prime Minister's National Council on Skill Development was constituted. NCSD was set up for giving policy directions and periodic review of efforts to address the issue of skill development by expansion of training capacity in a mission mode. The council was responsible for vision setting and laying down broad strategies for skill development.

The main functions of NCSD were as under:

1. To lay down overall broad policy objectives, financing and governance models and strategies relating to skill development.
2. To review the progress of schemes, and guide on mid-course corrections, additions and closure of parts or whole of any particular programme/scheme.
3. To coordinate public sector/private sector initiatives in a

framework of a collaborative action.

NCSD had set a target of creating 500 million skilled persons by 2022 with emphasis on inclusivity so as to deal with divides of gender, rural/urban, organized/unorganized, employment and traditional/contemporary work place. It had laid down the core governing principles and operating strategies for skill development.

Some of the key governance principles for skill development strategy included designing of programmes under which the learner could pay the skill provider directly, skills were fungible and bankable, individuals were enabled to convert their knowledge and skills through adequate testing and certification into higher diplomas and degrees. The emphasis was on promoting multiple models of delivery that could respond to differing situations in various states and to utilize existing available infrastructure of educational institutions for skill development after school hours without affecting formal education. The State Governments were encouraged to set up the State-level coordination body for skill development.

**3.5.2 National Skill Development Coordination Board (NSDCB):** In pursuance of the decision of the Cabinet at its meeting held on May 15, 2008 on Coordinated Action for Skill Development and setting up of the National Skill Development Corporation, National Skill Development Coordination Board was constituted.

NSDCB was entrusted with the coordination and harmonization of the initiatives of Governments for skill development spread across 17 Central Ministries and State Governments with the initiatives of the National Skill Development Corporation (NSDC). It had 12 members which included high level government officials and distinguished academicians.

The main functions of NSDCB included the following:

1. Enumerating strategies to implement the decisions of the Prime Minister's National Council on Skill Development (NCSD).

2. Developing suitable operational guidelines and instructions to achieve the objectives of skill development requirement of the economy.
3. Initiating solutions and strategies to address the problems of: (a) regional imbalance in skill development infrastructure, (b) socio-economic, rural-urban and gender divide, (c) quality teachers (d) ensuring effective utilization of investment in terms of money and infrastructure, (e) integrating varying existing regulatory institutions, (f) involving private sector to develop skills for wage/self-employment and (g) promoting apprenticeship/on-the-job training for creation of skilled personnel to address unemployment problem.
4. Encouraging State Governments to put in place similar institutional structures.
5. Establishing national skill inventory and national database for skill deficiency mapping on national web portal to facilitate exchange of information between prospective employers and job seekers.
6. Coordinating and facilitating the repositioning of employment exchanges as outreach points for storing and providing information on employment and skill development.
7. Coordinating the establishment of a credible accreditation system and a guidance framework for all accrediting agencies of different ministries and private players.
8. Monitoring, evaluating and analyzing the outcomes of the various schemes and programmes and apprising NCSD.

NSDCB had constituted the following 5 sub-committees to look into various aspects of skill development.

1. Curriculum revision.
2. Remodelling apprenticeship training.
3. Evolving vision on the status of vocational education and training in educational system.
4. Institutional mechanism for skill mapping and skill inventory on real time basis.
5. Improvement in accreditation and certification system.

**3.5.3 National Skill Development Corporation (NSDC):** See section 7.2 of chapter 7 of this book.

## 3.6 National Policy on Skill Development (NPSD), 2009

NPSD was formulated by the Ministry of Labour and Employment and was approved by the Cabinet in its meeting held on February 23, 2009. The objective of NPSD was to create a workforce empowered with improved skills, knowledge and internationally recognized qualifications to gain access to decent employment and ensure India's competitiveness in the dynamic global labour market. It aimed at increase in productivity of workforce both in the organized and the unorganized sectors, seeking increased participation of youth, women, disabled and other disadvantaged sections and to synergize efforts of various sectors and reform the present system. The salient features of NPSD were as under:

1. Demand-driven system guided by labour market signals thereby reducing skills mismatch.
2. Expansion of outreach using established as well as innovative approaches.
3. National vocational qualifications framework which, inter alia, included opportunities for horizontal and vertical mobility between general and technical education, recognition and certification of competencies irrespective of mode of learning.
4. System to deliver competencies in line with nationally and internationally recognized standards.
5. Focus on new emerging occupations.
6. Focus on pre-employment training and life-long learning.
7. Adequate participation of women, disabled persons and disadvantaged groups including economically backward and minorities and enhancing their access to training and employment opportunities.
8. Stress on research, planning and monitoring.
9. Involvement of social partners, i.e. sharing of responsibility for management and financing of the system with all

stakeholders and provide greater space for public-private-partnership (PPP).

10. Promoting excellence.
11. Use of modern training technologies including distance learning, e-learning, web-based learning etc.
12. Skill upgradation of trainers, their quality assurance, and improvement of status.

NPSD, 2009 was superseded by National Policy for Skill Development and Entrepreneurship (NPSDE), 2015. See chapter 5 of this book.

### 3.7 Twelfth Five Year Plan (2012-17) on Skill Development

Highlighting the need for skill development, Twelfth Plan identified the following focus areas during the Plan period:

1. "Improving the outreach of the skill development, both quantitatively and qualitatively to bridge the divides, namely spatial, sectoral, regional and gender and so on.
2. Putting in place an institutional mechanism that is focused solely on skill development.
3. Putting in place necessary support mechanisms to enable the financial requirements/skill loans for poor students (Credit Guarantee Fund).
4. Development of national skill qualification framework, incorporating the standards developed by sector skill councils, and have in place a regulatory framework to oversee the functioning and ensure accountability of sector skill councils.
5. Improving quality and quantity by focusing on training of trainers.
6. Promoting public-private-partnership.
7. Greater interaction among industry, academia and skill providers to narrow the gap between the demand and supply of skilled manpower.
8. Focus on informal sector by finding a model that reaches out to the people, as the livelihood promoting institutions, Panchayati Raj Institutions and NGOs are engaged effectively.

9. Developing ICT-based real time labour market information system.
10. An outcome based approach which ensures that the employability created is manifested in immediate, measurable and tangible employment/self-employment of the trainees.
11. An online national register of the persons skilled, and their current engagement—to not only provide a national database to employers and all other stakeholders, but also to facilitate a transparent monitoring system.
12. Review labour laws which inhibit the hiring of short-term interns and trainees.
13. All employment exchanges to come online, and act as pro-active counselling and placement centres.
14. Activating state skill missions and making them nodal points for receiving most of the skill related funding from Centre.
15. Setting up of national skill registry having facility to link various data bases across Ministries and States to work as a platform to link people seeking training to trainers/sponsoring organizations and people having skills to prospective employers.
16. Improving focus of Ministries—like Social Justice and Empowerment (SJE), Tribal Affairs (TA), Minority Affairs, Women and Child Development (WCD), Development of North-Eastern Region (DONER) and so on—working for disadvantaged sections on skill development programmes so that much larger funding for skill development through them may be ensured". [2]

### Endnotes

1. Role and functions of these ministries are given in chapter 7 of this book.
2. Government of India, Planning Commission, *Twelfth Five Year Plan (2012-17)*, Volume III, Chapter 22, para 22.124.

# 4

# Special Target Groups for Skill Development

One of the biggest challenges of skill development in our country is that 93 percent of the workforce is in the unorganized/informal sector. Consequently it is difficult to map existing skills in the unorganised sector and gauge the skilling requirement in the sector. On the other hand, the rate of job growth in informal sector is estimated to be twice that in formal sector.

Women constitute almost half of the demographic dividend. The key challenge here is to increase their participation in the country's labour force, which is directly linked to economic growth of the country. Mainstreaming gender roles by skilling women in non-traditional roles and increasing gender sensitivity in the workplace will have a catalytic effect on productivity.

## 4.1 Skill Development for Unorganized Sector Workers

As per the survey carried out by the National Sample Survey Organization in the year 2009-10, the total employment, in both organized and unorganized sectors in the country was of the order of 46.5 crore comprising of around 2.8 crore in the organized sector and the balance 43.7 crore workers in the unorganized sector. Out of 43.7 crore workers in the unorganized sector, there are 24.6 crore workers employed in agricultural sector, about 4.4 crore in construction work and remaining in manufacturing and service. Thus, approximately 93 percent of India's workforce is in the unorganized sector.

The sector cuts across all economic activities and includes rural and urban areas. It contributes to about 60 percent of the country's GDP. Strengthening the skill base of the unorganized sector will improve productivity, working conditions, labour rights, social security and living standards.

Separate institutional mechanism should be explored to plan, implement and monitor the skill development efforts for the unorganised sector which, *inter alia*, include weavers, handloom workers, fishermen and fisherwomen, toddy tappers, leather workers, plantation labour, beedi workers.

**4.1.1 Meaning, Size and Characteristics of Unorganized Workers:** The unorganised sector is equated with the unprotected segment of the labour market where entry is free, labour turnover is high, wages are significantly lower, and the workers, generally, lack legal protection. This sector includes the self-employed, home-based workers, workers in small and tiny industries, agricultural labour etc. The basic point that one has to remember here is that this sector is not homogenous.

The First National Commission on Labour (1969) stated that unorganised labour was a group of workers who cannot be identified by a definition but could be described as those who have not been able to organise in pursuit of a common objective because of constraints such as: (a) casual nature of employment, (b) ignorance and illiteracy, (c) small size of establishments with low capital investment per person employed, (d) scattered nature of establishments and (e) superior strength of the employer operating singly or in combination.

The size of the unorganised sector labour has been growing because of shrinkage of employment in the organised sector as well as authority.

Unorganised workers, in both self-employed and wage employed categories, remain, by and large, legally unrecognised as workers, which implies that the existing laws related to minimum wages or social security are not applied to them. Besides the lack of legal recognition, lack of a designated *business place* also works to increase their vulnerability and exposes them to exploitation by the authorities. Further, the dispersed nature of workplace makes organisation of these workers and enterprises more difficult, further adding to their invisibility.

According to the final report of the National Commission for Enterprises in the Unorganised Sector (NCEUS) [Chairman: Arjun Sengupta] released in April 2009, workers in the unorganized (or informal) sector constitute more than 93 percent of the total workforce of India. Unorganized sector workers are those who do not have any job security, income security or social security and are therefore extremely vulnerable to exogenous shocks.

The workers in the informal economy are clearly the overwhelming proportion of the workforce and most of these suffer from various forms of insecurities and vulnerabilities. It follows that policies have to focus on improving their conditions. However, the extent to which policy should focus upon increasing the share of the workforce in the organized sector has been a matter of some debate.

Broadly, unorganized workers have concentrated in a small number of activity groups. Among men, most of the wage workers are engaged either in some kind of manufacturing, construction, trading or transport activities. Among women, most of the informal workers are engaged in either some kind of manufacturing, construction activities or just domestic services.

Casual workers constitute about one-fifth of the workers in the unorganized non-agricultural sector. Among the casual workers, more than half are engaged in the construction sector, followed by one-fifth in the manufacturing sector.

**4.1.2 Target Groups in the Unorganized Sector for Skill Development:** The target groups in the unorganized sector include, among others, the following:

1. Own-account workers.
2. Workers and apprentices in micro enterprises.
3. Unpaid family workers.
4. Casual labourers.
5. Home-based workers.
6. Peripatetic workers.
7. Migrant labourers.

8. Out of school youth and adults in need of skills.
9. Farmers and artisans in rural areas.

In order to encourage participation in skill development, entry barriers such as educational qualification, transportation, loss of wages, problem of language etc. should be suitably addressed.

**4.1.3 Training Providers:**

1. Various institutions including schools and public/private training institutions/civil society organizations/NGOs etc. should be encouraged to conduct skill development programmes for the unorganised sector.
2. Mobile training vans should also be deployed in rural and remote areas where training infrastructure is awfully deficient.
3. Skill development centres should conduct skill development programmes primarily to support services and unorganised sector.
4. Public training institutions need to be given greater managerial and academic autonomy to design and offer programmes that meet the requirements of local economy and specific target groups.
5. Flexible delivery strategy and patterns that suit the needs of the target groups, such as part/full time and on/off site training, should be adopted.
6. Training should be predominantly short-term to encourage participation.
7. Arrangements should be made for the testing and certification of skills acquired in non-formal and informal arrangements.

Limited access to human and physical capital among workers acts as a major constraint on access to employment, quality of employment or growth of self-employment activities. A substantial proportion of wage workers in agriculture and non-agriculture are either landless or land-poor. Self-employed in agriculture have better access to land ownership. In modern times, education is important to obtain gainful, productive and remunerative employment. Unorganized workers have the lowest level of education and literacy. Scheduled castes (SCs), scheduled tribes (STs) and Muslims are overwhelmingly concentrated in the unorganized sector and in self-employed activities to meet their livelihood needs.

## 4.2 Skill Development for Marginalized and Vulnerable Groups

**4.2.1 Equal Access to Skill Development:** Human development insists that everyone should enjoy a minimum level of security. In fact, a system should be built in which the State bears the responsibility for providing and ensuring an elementary or basic level of security, and leaves room for partly or wholly contributory schemes. This will mean that the responsibility to provide a floor will be primarily that of the State, and it will be left to individual citizens to acquire higher levels of security through assumption of responsibility and contributory participation.

The root cause of social insecurity in India is poverty and that is largely due to lack of adequate or productive employment opportunities. The pattern of economic development in India since Independence in 1947 has left in its trail a variety of inequalities which have caused socio-politico tensions. While the economy has performed well in terms of growth rate of gross domestic product (GDP), its performance in terms of human development indicators has been unsatisfactory.

Development and empowerment of scheduled castes (SCs), scheduled tribes (STs), other backward classes (OBCs), minorities, disabled and other social groups in order to bring them at par with the rest of society is a commitment enshrined in the Constitution. Policies of the Central and State Governments have tried to ensure equal rights, and access to benefits and resources to disadvantaged groups in society to enable them to develop their potential and capacities as agents of social change, through the process of planned development.

India's recent economic growth performance has, indeed,

been creditable. However, such growth must make a demonstrable difference to the lives of the poorest and most vulnerable citizens. India has the potential and the means to secure a reasonable standard of living for all of its citizens. The socio-economically disadvantaged—particularly women in rural areas—are yet to benefit from development efforts.

Equal access to skill development is essential for all social groups particularly women and disadvantaged section of society, to help them in securing decent employment and moving out of poverty. Removing barriers to access and addressing their specific needs are key elements in achieving inclusive growth.

Entry barriers such as educational qualification, transportation, loss of wages, language etc. should be addressed. While enhancing the opportunity of skill development for all, entry assessments should be deployed to channelize people with different profiles and needs into appropriate skill development programmes. Effort should be combined with a major initiative in raising awareness among the target groups about the benefit of skill development, employment and learning opportunities and also about support schemes that enable them to participate in training.

In addition to vocational skills, the provision of soft (or life) skills—including basic literacy, numeracy, occupational safety and health, hygiene, basic labour rights, team work and confidence building—should be made as an integral component of the curricula. This will also help in empowerment of vulnerable groups.

Skill development for employability is an important strategy in the fight against poverty. Accordingly, the poor should have a priority claim and easy access to opportunities for skill development. Efforts in this regard should aim at mitigating the impact of these economic barriers at different stages, as well as actively promote access of the poor to educational and skill development opportunities through specially designed schemes and measures. Such measures—

special coaching for competing in admission tests, provision of non-formal skill development opportunities and the expanded provision of scholarships, books and soft-loans—should be developed and implemented. Efforts should be made to better integrate skill development into broader poverty reduction programmes and to strengthen the existing skill development components of such programmes.

**4.2.2 Scheduled Castes (SCs):** According to 2011 Census, the scheduled castes constituted 16.6 percent of the Indian population. In the past, they have been socially ostracized, economically exploited and denied human dignity and a sense of self-worth. The socio-economic development and protection of SCs from discrimination and exploitation has been a high priority area from the very start of Independent India.

People belonging to SC communities are spread all over the country; almost 80 percent of them live in rural areas. They constitute more than one-fifth of the population of Uttar Pradesh, Punjab, Himachal Pradesh and West Bengal. The State of Punjab has the highest proportion of SCs to the State population. More than half the scheduled caste population is concentrated in the five States of Uttar Pradesh (35.1 million), West Bengal (18.4 million), Tamil Nadu (11.8 million), Andhra Pradesh (12.3 million) and Bihar (13.0 million).

**4.2.3 Scheduled Tribes (STs):** The population of scheduled tribes (STs) in India stood at 10.42 crore as per the 2011 Census. STs constitute 8.6 percent of the total population of the country with 91.7 percent of them living in rural areas and 8.3 percent in urban areas. The sex-ratio of ST population in 2001 was 978 which was much higher than the national average of 933. The proportion of the ST population to the total population had also increased from 6.9 percent in 1971 to 8.2 percent in 2001.

The proportion of STs to the total population in States/Union Territories was the highest in the North-eastern region of Mizoram (94.5 percent) and Lakshadweep (94.5

percent) followed by Nagaland (89.1 percent), Meghalaya (85.9 percent). Within major states, Chhattisgarh (31.8 percent) had the highest percentage followed by Jharkhand (26.3 percent) and Odisha (22.1 percent). Of the total ST population in the country, Madhya Pradesh accounted for the highest proportion of ST population (14.5 percent) followed by Maharashtra (10.2 percent), Odisha (9.7 percent), Gujarat (8.9 percent), Rajasthan (8.4 percent), Jharkhand (8.4 percent) and Chhattisgarh (7.8 percent). In fact, 68 percent of the country's Scheduled Tribes population lives in these seven States only.

**4.2.4 Other Backward Classes (OBCs):** Considerable confusion exists regarding the percentage of OBCs population in India's total population. The Second Backward Classes Commission headed by Shri B.P. Mandal (1980), basing its calculation on Census 1931, estimated that other backward classes (OBCs) constituted 52 percent of the population. Recently, NSSO 61st Round (July 2004 to June 2005) report on 'Employment and Unemployment Situation among Social Groups in India' gave an estimate of OBC to constitute 41 percent of the population.

Following measures are needed to help SCs, STs and OBCs to acquire skills and training.

1. Reservations applicable to these groups should be strictly enforced, with appropriate gender composition.
2. Existing schemes for benefiting these groups should be reviewed, strengthened and made more effective.
3. Efforts should be made to mobilize capabilities and expertise of civil society organizations.
4. New innovative schemes and measures should also be devised to ensure full and effective participation by these groups, as well as the accrual of real benefits from skill development initiatives.

**4.2.5 Minorities:** The Constitution of India contains special provisions for the socio-economic development of the SCs, STs and OBCs [Articles 15(4), 16(4) of Part III, Articles 46 of Part IV, and Articles 330-342 of Part XVI of the Indian

Constitution]. However, religious and linguistic minorities are excluded from the purview of these special provisions, though cultural and educational rights of the religious and linguistic minorities are regarded as fundamental rights under Articles 29 and 30 of Part III of the Constitution.

While the socio-economic development of the scheduled castes (SCs), scheduled tribes (STs) and other backward classes (OBCs) formed an important part of the post-Independence development policy, it was presumed that development of the religious and linguistic minorities would be taken care of by the general process of growth and development.

However, the socio-economic conditions of some minorities, particularly Muslims, are a cause for concern.

Following measures are needed to help minorities acquire skills and training.

1. Skill development opportunities for minority groups should be expanded, particularly in minority concentrated areas (MCAs).
2. Existing schemes benefiting these groups should be reviewed, strengthened and made more effective.
3. Efforts should be made to mobilize capabilities and expertise of civil society organizations.
4. Formalization of non-formal skill acquisition and transfer should also be promoted in traditional art and craft sectors.

**4.2.6 Persons with Disabilities [1]:** The Census 2001, enumerated persons with disabilities, at 2.13 percent of India's total population. According to Eleventh Five Year Plan (2007-12), "The percentage of disabled people among the total population of any country depends on the definition of *disability* in that particular country as well as the enumeration methodology and its accuracy. In India, the definition of disability used in the Census is very different from that in the Persons with Disabilities Act, 1995. There is an urgent need for both a credible definition and system of data collection relating to persons with disabilities. It can be reasonably assumed that persons with disabilities constitute anywhere between 5 to 6 percent of our total population". [2]

Following measures are needed to help them acquire skills and training.

1. The current level of participation of persons with disabilities in skill programmes is very low, despite guidelines of reserving 3 percent of the seats for them. The guidelines apply only to the government sector.
2. People with varying degrees of physical and mental disabilities should be provided with appropriate adjustment training and skills training to bring them in the economic mainstream and make them productive citizens.
3. Training should be integrated with efforts to secure appropriate employment opportunities. Programmes of public awareness and community participation need to be strengthened to promote demand for vocational training by people with disabilities as well as to facilitate their inclusion in the labour market.

**4.2.7 School Drop-outs and Child Labour:** School drop-outs refer to those who leave the schools before completing XII standard. Following measures are needed to help them acquire skills and training.

1. School education should be strengthened to reduce the school drop outs. The quality of school education should influence the effectiveness of skill development programme as a whole. This will lay solid foundation for young people to acquire employable skills and engage in continuous skill upgradation throughout their working life.
2. School education should be used as a tool to increase vocational awareness among the young people.
3. School drop-outs, child labour and out-of-school youth need to be given alternative education coupled with skill development opportunities to bring them into the economic and social mainstream.
4. Short-term, market-oriented, demand-driven programmes should provide a flexible delivery framework suited to the

characteristics and circumstances of the target group.

5. Multi-skilling, multi-entry and exit, and linkages to skill upgradation opportunities in the future, should characterize such programmes. Short-term employable skills need to be expanded greatly to cater to the large size of the group.
6. Formal educational requirements in accessing training should be reviewed in order to facilitate easy access.

### 4.3 Skill Development for Women Workers

Skill development for employability should be used as an agent of change in promoting women's employment. Women face a multitude of barriers in accessing skills and productive employment, remaining on the job due to effect of globalization or otherwise and advancing to higher level jobs, as well as returning to the labour market after a period of absence, for example, in raising children. A policy of non-discrimination need to be pursued vigorously to provide equal access for women to skill development and employment.

The problems of women workers in general and in the unorganised sector in particular deserve special emphasis and focus in view of their marginalised position within the class of workers. Even when women are not employed in the sense of contributing to the national output, a considerable share of their time is consumed by socially productive and reproductive labour. This is what is called the *double burden of work* that distinguishes women from men. For women workers in the informal economy, the double burden of combining the tasks of production and reproduction is even more arduous because they are already engaged in activities that require long hours to obtain a subsistence wage.

Thus, while women workers constitute a marginalised category within the class of workers in general, there are layers of subordination determined by structural factors such as the initial conditions of social status and economic sector to which they belong. This is quite evident in the case of women workers in the unorganised sector. There is greater disadvantage for women workers in general and those belonging to rural as well as scheduled castes (SCs)/scheduled tribes (STs) in particular. Apart from such inherited disadvantages as lower social position, a number of other factors also contribute to such a picture. These are their limited asset position, access to resources, and low level of education and skill. Education, and consequently some ability to acquire formal skills, could be a moderating force but this aspect presents a dismal picture. The overall situation of women workers calls for interventions of a promotional nature from different entry points but with a strong emphasis on education.

**4.3.1 Education and Women Empowerment:** There is an increased awareness that education is one of the most valuable means of achieving gender equality and the empowerment of women. Education is seen as a critical factor in breaking the inter-generational cycle of transmission of poverty. The power of education lies not just in imparting formal literacy, but rather in the acquisition of skills that enable access to multiple literacy—economic, legal, health, political and media etc.

Education is a key intervention in initiating and sustaining processes of empowerment. Good quality education can help women and marginalized communities to: (a) improve their status, (b) enable them to have greater access to information and resources and (c) challenge various forms of discrimination. Education helps strengthen democratic processes as it allows for greater and more equitable participation. Being educated leads to greater self-confidence and self-esteem. It enables engagement with development processes and institutions of governance from a position of strength. Poor women from socially disadvantaged communities are invariably not literate and therefore find themselves at a disadvantage when participating in development processes.

It is, however, important to recognise that while being literate or educated is necessary for empowerment, it does not automatically ensure it. For that a society needs an education system which is of good quality and promotes critical thinking.

From the perspective of gender this means that education and literacy should enable women and girls to critically analyse their situations, raise questions about their subordination and help them make informed choices. It is well-known that the institution of schooling is an important site for socialisation that actually reinforces rather than challenges patriarchy and gender discrimination. It is in this context that the content and pedagogy of education become critical considerations.

The focus of educational planning is generally on formal education but this is only one dimension of the educational provisioning, especially when needs of deprived women are under consideration and empowerment of women is the main objective. Though the content of education and classroom pedagogy are critical to altering gender and other social relations it has not been paid the attention it deserves. Efforts to make curricula gender-sensitive have been undertaken but can be considered initial attempts as they have remained largely at the level of removing stereotypes or increasing visibility and have not looked at gender in terms of social relations.

Problems related to the representation of marginalized communities continue to exist and contribute to the deep sense of alienation of these communities from the mainstream education system and a reason for children dropping out. Sexuality is addressed in a problematic manner in educational materials. It is either related to population or reproductive health or seen as a problem associated with promiscuity and shame. Classrooms need to be transformed into spaces that can help girls think critically. Discriminatory practices based on identity-based prejudices need to be monitored and stopped. Corporal punishment, which is wide spread, needs to be checked. The role of the teacher is naturally crucial in this context.

Women, though they make half the world's population, constitute the largest group which is excluded from the benefits of development. Work participation rate of women is much less than that of men. The multiple roles of women and the meagre ability to access resources and available assets are areas of concern. It is important to emphasise that women require adequate security and protection to be self-reliant.

Special attention has to be paid to women workers because of problems peculiar to them. Comparatively speaking, they are much less organised. They also suffer from certain social prejudices and physical disabilities.

**4.3.2 Adverse Effects of Globalization on Women:** With the growing globalization and liberalization of the economy as well as increased privatization of services, women as a whole have been left behind and not been able to partake of the fruits of success. Mainstreaming of women into the new and emerging areas of growth is imperative. This will require training and skill upgradation in emerging trades, encouraging more women to take up vocational training and employment in the boom sectors. This will also require women to migrate to cities and metros for work. Provision of safe housing, and other gender friendly facilities at work will need to be provided.

Another facet of globalization is related to the fact that many persons especially women will be severely affected with the advent of setting up of industrial parks, national highways, special economic zones (SEZs) etc. as huge tracts of farm land are likely to be acquired for this purpose. This would require massive resettlement of the displaced persons and their families. It is therefore essential that a viable resettlement policy and strategy is formulated and put in place immediately which clearly reflects the needs of women impacted by globalization/displacement.

With the removal of all quantitative restrictions on the import of various products, the self-employed women's groups, especially in the informal sector, have started facing competition from the low-priced imported consumer goods which are invading the Indian market. Although this has the imminent danger of displacing a large number of employed/self-employed women, but at the same time, the process of globalization has also opened up opportunities for women entrepreneurs for exporting their products to the markets all over the world. Globalization has thus opened up new challenges for the realization of the goal of women's empowerment. Hence, strategies should be designed to enhance the capacity of women and empower them to cope with the negative economic and social impacts of the globalization process.

Several studies have indicated that adverse consequences of globalisation are disproportionately borne by women. Increased mechanization leading to displacement of female unskilled workers, increased migration of male workers in traditionally women-dominated areas, increase in female-headed household due to migration of males are some of the trends established in various studies.

Globalization has presented new challenges for the realization of the goal of women's equality, the gender impact of which has not been systematically evaluated fully. However, it is evident that there is a need for re-framing policies for access to employment and equality of employment. Benefits of the growing global economy have been unevenly distributed leading to wider economic disparities, the feminization of poverty, increased gender inequality through deteriorating working conditions and unsafe working environment especially in the informal economy and rural areas. Strategies need to be designed to enhance the capacity of women and empower them to meet the negative social and economic impacts, which may flow from the globalization process.

With upgradation of skills, opportunities for employment of women exist in several areas such as health services, food processing and crafts. Key areas of concern include women in small subsistence farming households, women workers in garment and textiles who will face increased competition after the phasing out of the Multi Fibre Agreement in 2005, and women displaced by new technologies in sectors such as construction, which have traditionally absorbed large numbers of women.

With the onset of trade liberalisation, women in India today are linked to the global economy to a very significant extent, as producers, entrepreneurs, service providers, consumers and citizens. There is a need to identify capacity constraints and entry barriers that prevent women from securing gains from trade. Trade-related awareness and capacity building of the women stakeholders need to be prioritised.

The globalization process has, in some countries, resulted in policy shifts in favour of more open trade and financial flows, privatization of state-owned enterprises and in many cases lower public spending particularly on social services. This change has transformed patterns of production and accelerated technological advances in information and communication and affected the lives of women, both as workers and consumers. In a large number of countries, particularly in developing and least developed countries, these changes have also adversely impacted on the lives of women and have increased inequality. The gender impact of these changes has not been systematically evaluated. Globalization has also affected cultural values, lifestyles and forms of communication.

In countries with economies in transition women are bearing most of the hardships induced by the economic restructuring and being the first to lose jobs in times of recession. They are being squeezed out from fast growth sectors. Loss of childcare facilities due to elimination or privatization of state work places, increased need for older care without the corresponding facilities, continuing inequality of access to training for finding re-employment and to productive assets for entering or expanding businesses are current challenges facing women in these countries.

**4.3.3 Poor Implementation of Women-related Laws:** In a semi-industrialised country like India, the working class in destined to be one of the weaker sections of society. Moreover, society being male-dominated, female labour receives very poor recognition or value. Not that there are no statutory provisions. In fact, the Constitution of India provides equal rights and opportunities to both the genders. In addition there are specific provisions for protection and welfare of working women in many of the labour laws. However, most of these statutes do not cover the units in small and informal sectors which are the predominant workplaces of women.

Even where they are covered by the statutes, the poor enforcement practically nullifies the provisions. Moreover, there is another tragic factor that has to be noted. The very laws which are meant for working women are paradoxically turned against their interests by unscrupulous employers. If the employers find it difficult to bypass these provisions, they get rid of the women workers and thus strike at the economic base of their livelihood. All these factors need to be studied in depth while drafting policy and legal provisions for the working women in order to plug all possible loopholes.

For the reasons mentioned above, as also for the benefit of working women,. their union leaders—and for all those who are interested in the welfare of women workers—knowledge of existing provisions of labour laws is very essential. Women's emancipation is part of India's general developmental plans but government action can be neither effective nor adequate unless women themselves become more aware of their rights and the corresponding responsibilities. Every woman is a working woman, whether she works in the home or outside it. Many women work to earn money. Working women must know that they have some basic rights which are given by the law.

Though India has created protective legislations for women, the enactments have not been easy to implement. The very vastness of the country, the scattered nature of women workers, their lack of education and legal literacy, indifferent attitude of bureaucracy and the general status of women in society have added to vulnerability of women. This is true not only of rural unorganised women, but to an extent of the urban women workers also.

Proactive measures that overcome barriers and facilitate participation, such as hostels for women, scholarships, transport, training materials and loans, should be made available on a large scale. Women's' vocational training programme should be expanded along with institutional network providing training facilities exclusively for women.

In order to promote skills and employability of women, the sectors which employ a large number of women need to be identified. These may include construction, home-based traditional crafts or piece rate work, financial and health services as well as agricultural sectors. Gender stereotyping in vocational courses should be eliminated to encourage women's participation in non-traditional occupations, including existing and emerging technological fields.

## Endnotes

1. Disabilities include orthopaedic, visual, hearing, speech and mental disabilities.
2. Government of India, Planning Commission, *Eleventh Five Year Plan* (2007-12), Volume I, p. 130.

# 5

# National Policy for Skill Development and Entrepreneurship (NPSDE), 2015

The Ministry of Labour and Employment, Government of India, had formulated a National Policy on Skill Development in 2009. The objective of this policy was to empower all individuals through improved skills, knowledge, nationally and internationally recognized qualifications to gain access to decent employment and ensure India's competitiveness in the global market.

On July 15, 2015, Prime Minister Shri Narendra Modi launched the National Policy for Skill Development and Entrepreneurship (NPSDE), 2015 along with the following three other landmark initiatives of the Ministry of Skill Development and Entrepreneurship:

- National Skill Development Mission.
- Pradhan Mantri Kaushal Vikas Yojana (PMKVY).
- Skill Loan Scheme.

The 2009 policy was, thus, superseded by NPSDE, 2015. The new policy tries to bring the world of education and training closer to the world of work so as to enable them together build a strong India.

The Ministry of Skill Development and Entrepreneurship, Government of India, is an integral part of the government policy on *Sabka Saath, Sabka Vikaas* and its commitment to overall human resources development to take advantage of the demographic profile of India in the coming years. The objective of NPSDE, 2015 is to meet the challenge of skilling at scale with speed and standard (quality). It aims to provide an umbrella framework to all skilling activities being carried out within the country, and to align them to common standards and link the skilling with demand centres.

In addition to laying down the objectives and expected outcomes, it also identifies the various institutional frameworks which can act as the vehicle to reach the expected outcomes. The national policy also provides clarity and coherence on how skill development efforts across the country can be aligned within the existing institutional arrangements. This policy links skills development to improved employability and productivity.

The salient features and provisions of NPSDE, 2015 are presented below.

### 5.1 Vision and Mission

**Vision:** To create an ecosystem of empowerment by skilling on a large scale at speed with high standards and to promote a culture of innovation based entrepreneurship which can generate wealth and employment so as to ensure Sustainable livelihoods for all citizens in the country.

**Mission:** The mission is to:

1. Create a demand for skilling across the country.
2. Correct and align skilling with required competencies.
3. Connect the supply of skilled human resources with sectoral demands.
4. Certify and assess in alignment with global and national standards.
5. Catalyse an ecosystem wherein productive and innovative entrepreneurship germinates, sustains and grows leading to creation of a more dynamic entrepreneurial economy and more formal wage employment.

### 5.2 Objectives of NPSDE, 2015

The core objective of NPSDE, 2015 is to empower the individuals by enabling them to realize their full potential through a process of lifelong learning where competencies are accumulated via instruments such as credible certifications, credit accumulation and transfer etc. As individuals grow, the society and nation also benefit from their productivity and growth. This will involve the following:

1. Make quality vocational training aspirational for both youth and employers whereby youth sees it as a matter of choice and employer acknowledges the productivity linked to skilled workforce by paying the requisite premium.
2. Ensure both vertical and horizontal pathways to skilled workforce for further growth by providing seamless integration of skill training with formal education.
3. Focus on an outcome-based approach towards quality skilling that on the one hand results in increased employability and better livelihoods for individuals, and on the other hand translates into improved productivity across primary, secondary and tertiary sectors.
4. Increase the capacity and quality of training infrastructure and trainers to ensure equitable and easy access to every citizen.
5. Address human resources needs by aligning supply of skilled workers with sectoral requirements of industry and the country's strategic priorities including flagship programmes like 'Make in India'.
6. Establish an IT-based information system for aggregating demand and supply of skilled workforce which can help in matching and connecting supply with demand.
7. Promote national standards in the skilling space through active involvement of employers in setting occupational standards, helping develop curriculum, providing apprenticeship opportunities, participating in assessments, and providing gainful employment to skilled workforce with adequate compensation. Operationalize a well-defined quality assurance framework aligned with global standards to facilitate mobility of labour.
8. Leverage modern technology to ensure scale, access and outreach, in addition to ease of delivering content and monitoring results.
9. Recognise the value of on-the-job training, by making apprenticeships in actual work environments an integral part

of all skill development efforts.

10. Ensure that the skilling needs of the socially and geographically disadvantaged and marginalized groups—like the scheduled castes (SCs), scheduled tribes (STs), other backward classes (OBCs), minorities, differently-abled persons—are appropriately taken care of.
11. Promote increased participation of women in the workforce through appropriate skilling and gender mainstreaming of training.
12. Promote commitment and ownership of all stakeholders towards skill development and create an effective coordination mechanism.

The core objective of the entrepreneurship framework is to coordinate and strengthen factors essential for growth of entrepreneurship across the country. This would include as under:

1. Promote entrepreneurship culture and make it aspirational.
2. Encourage entrepreneurship as a viable career option through advocacy.
3. Enhance support for potential entrepreneurs through mentorship and networks.
4. Integrate entrepreneurship education in the formal education system.
5. Foster innovation-driven and social entrepreneurship to address the needs of the population at the *bottom of the pyramid*.
6. Ensure ease of doing business by reducing entry and exit barriers.
7. Facilitate access to finance through credit and market linkages.
8. Promote entrepreneurship amongst women.
9. Broaden the base of entrepreneurial supply by meeting specific needs of both socially and geographically disadvantaged sections of the society including SCs, STs, OBCs, minorities, differently-abled persons.

## 5.3 Policy Framework for Skill Development: Eleven-point Strategy

The policy framework has been developed to accomplish the vision of 'Skill India' by adhering to the objectives mentioned above. The framework outlines the following 11 major paradigms and enablers to achieve these objectives of skilling India:

1. **Aspiration and Advocacy:** The need of the hour is to make skill development aspirational for boys and girls. For skill training to be looked at as a matter of choice, it must: (a) provide vertical growth pathways on the lines of the general education system, so that skill education and training is also seen as a valid route to earn degrees and diplomas, and consequently to positions of authority linked to such qualifications, (b) be associated with growth and sustainable livelihood pathways and (c) have a causal relationship with increased income for skilled workforce.
2. **Capacity:** The annual skilling in the country was estimated at around 7 million in 2014. In the current landscape, capacity is being created by private sector training organisations, industry in-house training, government and private industrial training institutes (ITIs), advanced training institutes (ATIs), tool rooms and in schools, colleges and polytechnics. For all existing and new capacity that will be generated, the focus will move from inputs to outcomes of skill training that include employability and placements of trainees. Incentives will be linked to placement in all training institutions. For Government supported schemes, funding will be linked to outcomes of the training programmes.
3. **Quality:** One-Nation-One-Standard should become the *mantra* to ensure that national standards and quality for skilling are globally aligned and Indian youth can aspire to secure local, national and international job opportunities. Quality of training can be measured by competency outcomes and employability of trainees. The following parameters have been identified for improving quality:

- Quality assurance framework embedded in NSQF. [1]

- Market relevant training programmes.
- Recognition of prior learning.
- Curriculum alignment.
- National certification framework.
- Employability skills.
- Placements.

4. **Synergy:** Skill development programmes being implemented by various Ministries/Departments/Agencies of the Central Government have different norms as regards the eligibility criteria, duration of training, maximum amount for training, outcomes, monitoring and tracking mechanism etc. This multiplicity of norms and parameters results in avoidable difficulties in implementation and makes it difficult to evaluate the performance of the skill development programmes across the Central Government in an objective manner.
5. **Mobilization and Engagement:** Industry needs to be closely involved in providing job opportunities to the skilled workforce. Industry will be encouraged to increasingly move towards employing only certified skilled people. In addition, employers need to rationalize the compensation paid across different levels of skills to award a skill premium for increased productivity as a result of higher skills.
6. **Global Partnerships:** The main objective of global partnerships and international collaborations is to leverage best practices from across the world. Such collaborations will immensely enrich domestic training programmes by enhancing their quality through learnings from successful international models of vocationalization of education, engaging with industry etc. Institutional arrangements through joint working groups, secretariats etc will be established for regular exchange of knowledge, experiences, research findings, teaching and learning materials, and innovations in skill development.
7. **Outreach:** The proposed KVKs will play a pivotal role in

identifying local employment opportunities and providing adequate training and post-training support according to needs of local areas such as migration support for skilled workers. The centres will also function as information centres for training and employment opportunities, as well as for various support schemes. KVKs in the form of mobile training facilities, will also be deployed to reach out to remote and difficult areas.

8. **ICT Enablement:** Promotion of only brick and mortar facilities will not ensure the speed and scale desired to transform the skill development efforts. The use of technology will be leveraged to scale up training facilities, enable access to remote areas and increase cost-effectiveness of delivery of vocational training. Government will also look to support innovative products, solutions and models that address critical gaps in skill ecosystem in an effective manner. Use of existing available networks such as the widespread optical fibre network will be optimized.
9. **Trainers and Assessors:** To achieve the massive target of skilling, it is of utmost importance to have quality trainers who are capable of training people in several fields. Similarly, quality assessors in sufficient numbers are also required to ensure consistent outcomes of assessment and certification process. Government will decisively intervene, directly or through other stakeholders, to bring more experienced people in training and assessment space, especially ex-servicemen in defence and retired/working people from industry.
10. **Inclusivity:** It is necessary to promote skill development initiatives that will ensure inclusivity, irrespective of gender, location, caste, sector etc. One of the key objectives is to safeguard the skilling needs of SCs, STs, OBCs, minorities, and differently-abled persons, as well as those living in difficult geographical pockets.
11. **Promotion of Skilling amongst Women:** According to Census Data 2001, women account for 48 percent of the

entire population in India. Women have the capability to further drive the economy of the country if their participation in the workforce is increased. With the help of skilling, women can have viable incomes, decent work and be major players who can contribute equally to the economic growth of the country.

### 5.4 Policy Framework for Entrepreneurship: Nine-point Strategy

The entrepreneurship policy framework has been developed to address the objectives. Vibrant entrepreneurship requires support from an enabling ecosystem of culture, finance, expertise, infrastructure, skills and business-friendly regulations. Many government and non-government organizations are playing enabling roles across each of these crucial supporting elements. This policy framework, cognizant of the need for the full ecosystem to be present to unlock entrepreneurial potential, proposes the following nine part entrepreneurship strategy:

1. **Educate and Equip Potential and Early Stage Entrepreneurs Across India:** In partnership with experts, a world class entrepreneurship education curriculum will be developed. Through a blend of online and experiential learning, potential entrepreneurs will go through hands-on, student-centric courses that help them acquire skills they need to start an enterprise. This curriculum will build on and adapt the best entrepreneurship education content available globally.
2. **Connect Entrepreneurs to Peers, Mentors and Incubators:** To support young entrepreneurs, a web and mobile-based platform connecting the entire entrepreneurial ecosystem will be established. Students, young entrepreneurs, mentors, incubators, funding agencies and basic service providers will all be able to log in and connect to each other in their respective industries and locations.
3. **Support Entrepreneurs through Entrepreneurship Hubs (E-Hubs):** Support to entrepreneurs, including

coordinated delivery of national and state government entrepreneurship programmes and access to enabling resources, a national network of entrepreneurship hubs (E-Hubs) will be established.

4. **Catalyse a Culture Shift to Encourage Entrepreneurship:** To promote entrepreneurship, state and national level interaction with stakeholders will be convened. Keynote speakers from industry, both domestic and international, will be invited to share best practice from the field. International linkages will also be established through internship opportunities and exchange trips to global entrepreneurship hubs such as Silicon Valley and Israel.
5. **Encourage Entrepreneurship among Under-represented Groups:** Special focus will be given to the inclusion of scheduled castes and scheduled tribes, minorities, differently-abled, etc. and regionally under-represented areas including large part of Eastern and North-Eastern India in entrepreneurship programmes.
6. **Promote Entrepreneurship amongst Women:** The Economic Survey conducted for India by OECD in November 2014 clearly enlists low female economic participation as one of the major findings. Creating more and better employment for women has high growth potential. Currently, the contribution of women in workforce is limited to only 24 percent. Head of UN Women has also indicated that India's GDP will leapfrog by another 4.2 percent if women in India can contribute their full potential to the economy.
7. **Improve Ease of Doing Business:** A business-friendly environment with easy entry and exit procedures will encourage entrepreneurial activity. The following actions to rationalise business procedures and regulations through the following initiatives should be investigated:

- Introduce unique enterprise number (UEN) that a new enterprise could use for various registrations including taxes, labour laws and social security. Once UEN is available, all regulatory and support agencies shall use it to fasten the process of setting up an enterprise.

- Introduce an online composite application form (CAF) that will help entrepreneurs file a single application for obtaining all approvals and clearances from various government authorities.
- Encourage states to strengthen existing single window system with a high power committee empowered to give all necessary clearances for setting up a business.
- Convert the present district industries centres (DICs) into business development centres (BDCs) with an objective to provide technical and procedural hand-holding support and counselling to pre-start-up, nascent, early start-up and growth ventures.
- Permit flexibility to start-ups in hiring and retaining workforce for operational adjustments and rationalisation during the first 3 years of operation of an enterprise, assuming that by the end of 3 years it will either stabilise and grow or become sick and close down.
- Allow easy exit to enterprises if they have been in operation for less than 3 years. Such enterprises will be facilitated to close their operations, if not found viable, within a period of 3 months. Special fast track court would be set-up to expedite the process of closure of such firms.
- Consider tax incentives to new and existing entrepreneurs.

8. **Improve Access to Finance:** As per RBI data, the share of small-scale industries in gross bank credit from scheduled commercial banks has been continuously decreasing. Its share has fallen from 15.42 percent of the gross bank credit in 1991 to 6.34 percent in 2006-07. To reinvigorate the flow of credit to deserving entrepreneurs, the following interventions could be considered:

- Ensure that credit delivery norms are met by financial institutions without compromising the quality of the projects submitted for credit.
- Strengthen venture capital companies in quasi-public

sector by infusing capital through equity participation.

- Incentivise Angel financing by providing appropriate rebates on capital gains made by investors.
- Promote a *rescue* culture by revisiting bankruptcy rules and facilitate counselling and advisory services to troubled firms by appropriately addressing legal status.
- Encourage national and state bodies, viz. National Scheduled Caste Finance and Development Corporation (NSCFDC), National Minorities Development and Finance Corporation (NMDFC), National Backward Classes Finance and Development Corporation (NBCFDC), to provide credit to micro enterprise start-ups launched by their target population.
- Explore the possibility of setting up a national fund for the unorganised sector, as recommended by the National Commission for Enterprises in the Unorganised Sector in 2007, to hasten the process of achieving inclusive growth of entrepreneurship.
- Encourage and support financial institutions to develop innovative micro-level financial tools to enhance investibility in micro ventures. Further, they would also be encouraged to increase lending in rural areas through self-help groups and innovative micro-financing.

9. **Foster Social Entrepreneurship and Grassroots Innovations:** Social enterprises have emerged as important business instruments to address the issues of poverty, unemployment and inequity in society, through socially-oriented business innovations. Social innovation seeks to answer these social problems by offering new products and services which allow the poor to interact with markets as active participants rather than passive recipients. Considering the need to encourage such social enterprises, the following will be undertaken:

- Encourage universities and academic institutions to launch a course on social entrepreneurship, including online distance education, to actively promote social entrepreneurship.

- Foster a social capital market place by offering fiscal incentives to attract investors and make provision for funding support under a separate scheme(s) like social venture fund, to facilitate social entrepreneurs' access to credit.
- Facilitate creation of social enterprises even with a modest capital base, through social incubates across the country.
- Encourage innovators, universities and institutions to patent innovative entrepreneurship ideas and technologies by promoting and strengthening intellectual property rights (IPRs).
- Create grassroots technology innovation hubs to harness the innovation potential of grassroots innovators.
- Promote and encourage grassroots innovations and assist innovators to commercialise and up-scale their products and services.
- To encourage innovation, collaborate with organisations such as the National Innovation Foundation to encourage grassroots technological innovation and integrate with the national research and innovation ecosystem. Using the national network of E-Hubs and other platforms, assist entrepreneurs in commercializing and scaling up their products and services.

### 5.5 Governance Structure and Financing

**5.5.1 Governance Structure:** Ministry of Skill Development and Entrepreneurship has been created to fulfil the vision of a Skilled India where human resources development is the primary focus. MSDE will be responsible for co-ordination with all concerned for evolving an appropriate skill development framework, removal of disconnect between demand for, and supply of, skilled manpower, skill upgradation, building of new skills, innovative thinking and talents for existing and future jobs. MSDE will also play the lead role in ensuring the implementation of the National Policy for Skill Development and Entrepreneurship, 2015.

Skill development and entrepreneurship are

complementary to each other. The key stakeholders include Central Ministries/Departments, State Governments, and industry/employers. There is a need to ensure alignment of the efforts of all stakeholders in skill and entrepreneurship landscape towards a common goal. While MSDE will co-ordinate and converge all efforts in this space, the relevant Central Ministries/Departments, State Governments and industry/employers are expected to fulfil the roles and responsibilities pertaining to their domain as laid down in the National Policy for Skill Development and Entrepreneurship.

The objectives and targets under the National Policy will be met in mission mode approach. The National Skill Development Mission will be launched to implement and co-ordinate all skilling efforts in the country towards the objectives laid down in the policy. The Mission will be housed in MSDE and the key institutional mechanisms for achieving the objectives of the Mission will be divided into a three-tier structure at the Centre to steer, drive and execute the Mission's objectives. The Mission will consist of a governing council at apex level, a steering committee and a mission directorate (along with an Executive Committee) as the executive arm of the Mission. At State level, States will be encouraged to create State Skill Development Missions (SSDM) along the lines of National Skill Development Mission with a steering committee and mission directorate at State level. States will, in turn, be supported by district committees at the functional tier.

Mission directorate will be supported by three other institutions: National Skill Development Agency (NSDA), National Skill Development Corporation (NSDC), and Directorate General of Training (DGT) all of which will have horizontal/vertical linkages with Mission Directorate to facilitate smooth functioning of the national institutional mechanism.

**5.5.2 National Skill Development Agency (NSDA):** NSDA was set up as a Society in June 2013. NSDA will focus on the two verticals of quality assurance and policy research in the skills space. It will be chiefly responsible for the following activities:

1. Operationalise and implement National Skills Qualification Framework (NSQF).
2. Establish and operationalise a QA framework embedded in NSQF to improve consistency of outcomes in the skills landscape, which will include laying down a framework for training, assessment and certification processes and agencies in the country.
3. Operationalise National Skills Qualification Committee (NSQC) to meet its objectives.
4. Design and implement the National Labour Market Information System.
5. Develop national protocols for registration and accreditation of private training providers.
6. Promote use of Skill India logo on skill certificates by SSCs/agencies adhering to the QA framework.
7. Anchor Prime Minister's Skill Development Fellow Programme.

National Skills Research Division (NSRD), under NSDA will be established to serve as the apex division for providing technical and research support to the Mission. This division will act as a think-tank for MSDE and be the core skill development hub, which will connect implementation of the Mission with academic research and data. Its 4 key functions will include research, policy advisory/inputs, career support and knowledge exchange networks.

**5.5.3 National Skill Development Corporation (NSDC):** NSDC, a public private partnership was set up in 2008 as a Section 25 company under Companies Act, 1956 with shareholding of Government of India at 49 percent and that of the private sector at 51 percent. It will be the nodal organization for all private sector initiatives in the short-term skilling space. Its mandate will primarily include the following:

1. Catalyse the creation of market-based, scalable business

by providing funding through a combination of debt, equity and grants.

2. Implementing skills voucher programme.
3. Driving engagement with industry and businesses.
4. Promote centres of excellence for training of trainers in coordination with States and SSCs.
5. Initiating and incubating sector skills councils (SSCs).
6. Discharge any other function as may be assigned to it by the Ministry.

**5.5.4 Directorate General of Training:** The two verticals of training and apprenticeship training under DGET, MoLE have been shifted to MSDE from April 16, 2015. Its large institutional framework consisting of ITIs, ATIs, RVTIs and other national institutes will act as tools of execution for Mission activities. Other functions will include the following:

1. Setting up framework for structure of courses, assessment, curricula creation, affiliation and accreditation of institutes, under NCVT.
2. Develop national standards on syllabi, equipment, scale of space, duration of courses and methods of training.
3. Advise on training policy in its network of training institutes.
4. Co-ordinate functioning of industrial training institutes (ITIs).
5. Run training programmes for training of trainers and instructors.
6. Run special institutes for training of women.
7. Leverage field infrastructure for strong industry interface in all facets of training, including on-the-job training.
8. Provide technical support to vocational education across the country.
9. Anchor and operationalise Apprentices Act, 1961 as overhauled by comprehensive amendments in December 2014.
10. Operationalise various training schemes through ITIs and vocational training providers (VTPs).

**5.5.5 Sector Skill Councils (SSCs):** In order to ensure that skill development efforts being made by all stakeholders in the system are in accordance with actual needs of industry, SSCs are being set up. SSCs are industry-led and industry-governed bodies, which will help link the requirements of industry with appropriately trained manpower.

SSCs will discharge the following functions:

1. Identification of skill development needs including preparing a catalogue of types of skills, range and depth of skills to facilitate individuals to choose from them.
2. Development of a sector skill development plan and maintenance of skill inventory.
3. Determining skills and competency standards and qualifications and getting them notified as per NSQF.
4. Standardization of affiliation, accreditation, examination and certification process in accordance with NSQF as determined by NSQC. May also conduct skill-based assessment and certification for QP/NOS-aligned training programmes.
5. Participation in the setting up of affiliation, accreditation, examination and certification norms for their respective sectors.
6. Plan and facilitate the execution of training of trainers along with NSDC and States.
7. Promotion of academies of excellence.
8. Lay special emphasis on the skilling needs of STs/SCs, differently-abled and minority populations.
9. SSCs shall ensure that the persons trained and skilled in accordance with the norms laid down by them are assured of employment at decent wages.

**5.5.6 Entrepreneurship Institutes:** National Institute for Entrepreneurship and Small Business Development (NIESBUD) and Indian Institute of Entrepreneurship (IIE), Guwahati were transferred to MSDE on May 2, 2015. NIEBUD is a society engaged in training, consultancy, research and publication, in order to promote entrepreneurship.

It is operating from an integrated campus in NOIDA, Uttar Pradesh, and its major activities include training, conducting research/evaluation studies, developing course curricula for entrepreneurship development programmes, undertaking development programmes in clusters, running an incubation centre etc.

IIE's objectives include promotion and development of entrepreneurship, conducting research, providing consultancy for entrepreneurship development, providing consultancy and monitoring service to MSMEs/potential entrepreneurs and enhancing employability of participants. Further, a national advisory committee comprising of representatives/members from all relevant Ministries/Departments, industry, academia, specialized institutions, funding agencies and young entrepreneurs engaged in promoting entrepreneurship etc. will be set up to institutionalise entrepreneurship development in the country.

**5.5.7 Financing:** Public funds (funding by Central Government, State Governments and grant-based schemes) are finite and will not be able to cover the magnitude of the challenge of Skilling India. Hence, alternative sources of funds are required. Therefore, all stakeholders, the Government, both at Centre and States, public and private enterprises, and the direct beneficiary (the individual), would contribute in mobilizing financial or in-kind resources for skill development. The success of the policy will depend upon the quantum of resources mobilised from all stakeholders.

National Skill Development Fund (NSDF) has been set up by Government of India with the objective of encouraging skill development in the country. A Public Trust set up by Government of India is the custodian of the Fund. The Fund acts as a receptacle for all donations, contribution in cash or kind from all contributors (including Government, multilateral organizations, corporations etc.) for furtherance of the objectives of the Fund.

To channelize the interest of a plethora of organisations to participate in the mission of Skill India, a strategic vehicle to create a multiplier effect on skilling has been devised. A 'Resource Optimization for Skilling at Scale Platform' has been proposed by the Government to act as a demand-responsive and flexible vehicle to tackle the issues of skills shortages through skill development, job creation and placement at scale. It will serve as the aggregator vehicle for pooling the funds of multilateral agencies, companies, foundations, NGOs and individuals for skilling interventions by leveraging existing infrastructure and resources. The platform will also be subjected to timely audits to ensure that the contributions are used for the intended purpose.

To attract funds from industry, companies will be encouraged to spend at least 25 percent of their corporate social responsibility (CSR) funds on skill development initiatives directly or through NSDF. Further, industry should earmark at least 2 percent of its payroll bill (including for contract labour) for skill development initiatives in their respective sectors. These funds can be channelized for skill development activities either through respective SSCs or through NSDF.

All Government schemes across sectors will be encouraged to apportion a certain percentage (10 percent) of the scheme budget towards skilling of human resources in local regions in the required sector. These funds could be used for implementation directly or be routed through NSDF. Government may consider other options including cess etc. to raise funds for meeting the requirements of this sector.

End-user funding through a basic fee paying model will also be a key medium for funding training activities. However, the Government believes that the inability to pay training costs should not stop any desirous citizen in the country from acquiring any certified skill training. The Government will promote grant of scholarships, rewards and skill vouchers (SV) for funding of training costs. It will also be ensured that for all government schemes, Direct Benefit Transfer (DBT) will be used as a mechanism for payment disbursement.

A Credit Guarantee Fund for skill development and a National Credit Guarantee Trustee Company (NCGTC) has been set up to support the initiative of loans for the purpose of skilling and will be used to leverage credit financing in the skill landscape. It will be further expanded to ensure greater outreach and access to all citizens. Similarly, a Credit Guarantee Fund for Entrepreneurship Development worth ₹ 3,000 crore per year has already been initiated under Prime Minister MUDRA Yojana through NCGTC.

**5.6 Monitoring and Evaluation**

The National Policy for Skill Development and Entrepreneurship has been structured as an outcome-oriented policy. It is, therefore, desirable that there should be regular monitoring and evaluation of the initiatives to ensure that best practices can be scaled and corrective measures can be introduced. The main idea of having a robust monitoring and evaluation mechanism is to ensure successful implementation of the policy initiatives.

Government desires to set up a policy implementation unit (PIU) so as to review the implementation and progress of the various initiatives under this policy. The PIU will be housed in MSDE with Secretary as the Chairperson and representation from NITI Aayog. For the smooth functioning of the PIU, it will also ensure constant consultation with stakeholders to get feedback so as to enable improvements, if required.

The PIU will perform the following functions:

1. List all the action points as mentioned in the policy on which further action is required.
2. Identify all the agencies involved and map the actionable points to the responsible agency.
3. Co-ordinate with all the agencies involved and help them devise a draft outline as well as timelines for the implementation of the initiatives assigned to them.
4. Timelines that are explicitly mentioned in the policy for certain initiatives will supersede other timelines.

5. Act as a co-ordinating body for all the implementing agencies and support them to enhance their efficiency.
6. PIU will also conduct monthly review of the action points and nudge them if the progress is not as expected.

PIU will be made responsible to the NSDM. It will present its reports, findings and the way forward to the Steering Committee of the Mission every quarter. PIU will be the main body overlooking the implementation of policy.

**5.6.1 Impact Assessment:** For the purpose of undertaking impact assessment, annual as well as 5 year targets will be set for each stakeholder by the PIU. Impact assessment will be undertaken to ensure that the targets are met well within the time frame. The stakeholders will also be subject to a quarterly review. For the purpose of impact assessment, the following monitoring indicators, amongst others, are prescribed:

1. Number/registrations of youth interested in skilling.
2. Number of youth registered in training programmes.
3. Number of youth assessed and certified by regulatory authorities.
4. Placement rate of skilled trainees.
5. Number of accredited/affiliated training providers/centres.
6. Number of certified trainers, sector-wise.
7. Number of certified assessors, sector-wise.
8. Number of job roles for which QPs and NOS have been developed.
9. Existing public infrastructure leveraged for training.
10. Number of skilled persons engaged in overseas employment.
11. Reduction in sectoral demand and supply gap.
12. Amount of private funds mobilised for encouraging skill development and entrepreneurship.
13. Percentage of socially and geographically disadvantaged groups enrolled in training programmes.
14. Percentage of skilled youth who are self-employed.
15. Infrastructure dedicated for entrepreneurship support.
16. Number of schools with skills and entrepreneurship courses.

17. Percentage of socially and geographically disadvantaged groups engaged in self employment.

With the help of the PIU, it will be easier to monitor the implementation of the policy initiatives and take corrective measures in case of non-compliance. A mid-term review of the policy will be undertaken based on impact assessment by a third party. The policy can be considered for review after 5 years, based on learnings from implementation of the policy.

To sum up, NPSDE, 2015 has four thrust areas. It addresses key obstacles to skilling, including low aspirational value, lack of integration with formal education, lack of focus on outcomes, low quality of training infrastructure and trainers etc. Further, it seeks to align supply and demand for skills by bridging existing skill gaps, promoting industry engagement, operationalising a quality assurance framework, leverage technology and promoting greater opportunities for apprenticeship training.

Equity is also a focus of NPSDE, 2015, which targets skilling opportunities for socially/geographically marginalised and disadvantaged groups. Skill development and entrepreneurship programmes for women are a specific focus area. In the entrepreneurship domain, it seeks to educate and equip potential entrepreneurs, both within and outside the formal education system. It also seeks to connect entrepreneurs to mentors, incubators and credit markets, foster innovation and entrepreneurial culture, improve ease of doing business and promote a focus on social entrepreneurship.

The primary objective of NPSDE, 2015 is to meet the challenge of skilling at scale with speed, standard (quality) and sustainability. It aims to provide an umbrella framework to all skilling activities being carried out within the country, to align them to common standards and link skilling with demand centres. In addition to laying down the objectives and expected outcomes, it also identifies the overall institutional framework which will act as a vehicle to reach the expected outcomes. Skills development is the shared responsibility of the key stakeholders, viz. Government, the entire spectrum of corporate sector, community-based organizations, highly qualified and dedicated individuals, industry and trade organisations and other stakeholders.

NPSDE, 2015 links skill development to improved employability and productivity in paving the way forward for inclusive growth in the country. The skill strategy is complemented by specific efforts to promote entrepreneurship in order to create ample opportunities for the skilled workforce.

**Endnote**

1. NSQF is an important institutional mechanism that ensures consistency of nationally recognized qualifications both for formal and non-formal skills-based education and training. It accommodates experiential life-long learning through mechanisms such as recognition of prior learning, improves the alignment of formal and non-formal training programmes with industry requirements; and increases options for students by broadening programme and progression for learners through horizontal and vertical pathways.

# 6

# National Skill Development Mission (NSDM), 2015 and Initiatives

## 6.1 Why are Skills and Knowledge Important for India?

Skills and knowledge are the driving forces of economic growth and social development for any country. India currently faces a severe shortage of well-trained, skilled workers. It is estimated that only 2.3 percent of the workforce in India has undergone formal skill training as compared to 68 percent in the UK, 75 percent in Germany, 52 percent in USA, 80 percent in Japan and 96 percent in South Korea. [1]

Large sections of the educated workforce have little or no job skills, making them largely unemployable. Therefore, India must focus on scaling up skill training efforts to meet the demands of employers and drive economic growth.

India's annual skilling capacity was estimated at approximately 7 million during the period 2013-2014. Apart from meeting its own demand, India has the potential to provide a skilled workforce to fill the expected shortfall in the ageing developed world. India is one of the youngest nations in the world, with more than 54 percent of the total population below 25 years of age and over 62 percent of the population in the working age group (15-59 years). The country's population pyramid is expected to bulge across the 15-59 age group over the next decade.

This demographic advantage is predicted to last only until 2040. India therefore has a very narrow timeframe to harness its demographic dividend and to overcome its skill shortages. The enormity of India's skilling challenge is further aggravated by the fact that skill training efforts cut across multiple sectors and require the involvement of diverse stakeholders such as: (a) multiple government departments at the centre and state levels, (b) private training providers, (c) educational and training institutions, (d) employers, (e) industry associations and (f) assessment and certification bodies and trainees. All these stakeholders need to align their work together in order to achieve the target of Skill India.

### 6.2 Launching of Skill India Mission

National Skill Development Mission (NSDM) was approved by the Union Cabinet on July 1, 2015, and officially launched by the Prime Minister on July 15, 2015 on the occasion of World Youth Skills Day. 18,000 plus ITI graduating students received job offer letters on the occasion of World Youth Skills Day. Government has set a target to provide skill training to 40.02 crore people by 2022.

On the same day (July 15, 2015), the Prime Minister launched the following other three landmark initiatives of the Ministry of Skill Development and Entrepreneurship:

1. National Policy for Skill Development and Entrepreneurship (NPSDE), 2015. [2]
2. Pradhan Mantri Kaushal Vikas Yojana (PMKVY).
3. Skill Loan Scheme.

NSDM has been developed to create convergence across sectors and States in terms of skill training activities. Further, to achieve the vision of Skilled India, NSDM would not only consolidate and co-ordinate skilling efforts, but also expedite decision making across sectors to achieve skilling at scale with speed and standards. It will be implemented through a streamlined institutional mechanism driven by Ministry of Skill Development and Entrepreneurship (MSDE).

The Ministry of Skill Development and Entrepreneurship (earlier Department of Skill Development and Entrepreneurship, first created in July 2014) was set up in November 2014 to drive the Skill India agenda in a Mission Mode in order to converge existing skill training initiatives and combine scale and quality of skilling efforts, with speed.

The Ministry, therefore, launched NSDM which will

provide the overall institutional framework to rapidly implement and scale up skill development efforts across India. It seeks to provide the institutional capacity to train a minimum of 300 million skilled people by the year 2022.

**6.3 Objectives of NSDM**

NSDM seeks to:

1. Create an end-to-end implementation framework for skill development, which provides opportunities for life-long learning. This includes incorporation of skilling in the school curriculum, providing opportunities for quality long and short-term skill training, by providing gainful employment and ensuring career progression that meets the aspirations of trainees.
2. Align employer/industry demand and workforce productivity with trainees' aspirations for sustainable livelihoods, by creating a framework for outcome focused training.
3. Establish and enforce cross-sectoral, nationally and internationally acceptable standards for skill training in the country by creating a sound quality assurance framework for skilling, applicable to all Ministries, States and private training providers.
4. Build capacity for skill development in critical unorganized sectors (such as the construction sector, where there are few opportunities for skill training) and provide pathways for re-skilling and up-skilling workers in these identified sectors, to enable them to transition into formal sector employment.
5. Ensure sufficient, high quality options for long-term skilling, benchmarked to internationally acceptable qualification standards, which will ultimately contribute to the creation of a highly skilled workforce.
6. Develop a network of quality instructors/trainers in the skill development ecosystem by establishing high quality teacher training institutions.

7. Leverage existing public infrastructure and industry facilities for scaling up skill training and capacity building efforts.
8. Offer a passage for overseas employment through specific programmes mapped to global job requirements and benchmarked to international standards.
9. Enable pathways for transitioning between the vocational training system and the formal education system, through a credit transfer system.
10. Promote convergence and co-ordination between skill development efforts of all Central Ministries, Departments, States, and implementing agencies.
11. Support weaker and disadvantaged sections of society through focused outreach programmes and targeted skill development activities.
12. Propagate aspirational value of skilling among youth, by creating social awareness on value of skill training.
13. Maintain a national database, known as the Labour Market Information System (LMIS), which will act as a portal for matching the demand and supply of skilled workforce in the country. The LMIS, will on the one hand provide citizens with vital information on skilling initiatives across the country. On the other, it will also serve as a platform for monitoring the performance of existing skill development programmes, running in every Indian state.

### 6.4 Institutional Mechanisms

Key institutional mechanisms for achieving the objectives of NSDM have been divided into three tiers. NSDM will consist of a Governing Council at apex level, a Steering Committee, and a Mission Directorate as the executive arm of the Mission.

Mission Directorate will be supported by three other institutions: National Skill Development Agency (NSDA), National Skill Development Corporation (NSDC), and Directorate General of Training (DGT)—all of which will have linkages with Mission Directorate to facilitate smooth functioning of the national institutional mechanism. These three agencies would continue to lie under the umbrella of Ministry of Skill Development and Entrepreneurship.

At State level, States will be encouraged to create State Skill Development Missions (SSDM) along the lines of National Skill Development Mission with a Steering Committee and Mission Directorate at State level. States will, in turn, be supported by District Committees at the functional tier.

### 6.5 NSDM Strategy

Seven sub-missions have been proposed initially to act as building blocks for achieving overall objectives of NSDM. They are:

1. Institutional training.
2. Infrastructure.
3. Convergence.
4. Trainers.
5. Overseas employment.
6. Sustainable livelihoods.
7. Leveraging public infrastructure.

The sub-missions can be added to/amended as per decision of Governing Council. The power to identify sub-missions in crucial areas which require immediate attention will lie with Governing Council chaired by the Prime Minister. Executive guidelines and detailing of each sub-mission will be done by Executive Committee headed by Secretary, MSDE.

Key focus areas of the sub-missions include: (a) addressing the long-term and short-term skilling needs through revamp of existing institutional training framework and establishing new institutions, (b) undertaking sector-specific skill training initiatives, (c) ensuring convergence of existing skill development programmes, (d) leveraging existing public infrastructure for skilling, (e) focusing on training of trainers, (f) facilitating overseas employment, and (g) promoting sustainable livelihoods.

Sub-Missions have currently been proposed in priority areas. The number of sub-missions can be modified as per changing skill requirements and challenges. Each sub-mission will be headed by a Joint Secretary or Director level officer designated as CEO, sourced from the public or private sector, who has a solid track record of implementing projects and achieving targets in a timely manner. The Sub-Mission's support team will consist of high performing individuals drawn from the public and private domains.

### 6.6 Pradhan Mantri Kaushal Vikas Yojana (PMKVY)

On July 15, 2015, Prime Minister Shri Narendra Modi launched the Pradhan Mantri Kaushal Vikas Yojana (PMKVY), 2015 along with the following three other landmark initiatives of the Ministry of Skill Development and Entrepreneurship:

1. National Policy for Skill Development and Entrepreneurship, 2015.
2. National Skill Development Mission.
3. Skill Loan Scheme.

The slogan *Kaushal Bharat, Kushal Bharat* suggests that skilling Indians (*Kaushal Bharat*) will result in a happy, healthy, prosperous and strong nation (*Kushal Bharat*).

PMKVY is the flagship, demand-driven, reward-based skill training scheme of the Ministry of Skill Development and Entrepreneurship (MSDE). It is intended to incentivise skill training by providing financial rewards to candidates who successfully complete approved skill training programmes. For the first time, the skills of young people who lack formal certification, such as workers in India's vast unorganised sector, will be recognised. Through an initiative known as recognition of prior learning (RPL), 10 lakh youth will be assessed and certified for the skills that they already possess.

Under PMKVY, skill cards and skill certificates are awarded which allow trainees to share their skill identity with employers. Each skill card and skill certificate features a quick response code (QR Code), which can be read through a QR reader on mobile devices. Trainees can use these to share their skill qualifications with employers in a quick and reliable way during the job search process.

Approved for another four years (2016-2020) to benefit 10 million youth, training and assessment fees under PMKVY are completely paid by the Government.

**6.6.1 Key Components of the Scheme:** These are as under:

**A. Short-term Training:** Short-term training imparted at PMKVY Training Centres (TCs) is expected to benefit candidates of Indian nationality who are either school/college dropouts or unemployed. Apart from providing training according to the National Skills Qualification Framework (NSQF), TCs shall also impart training in soft skills, entrepreneurship, financial and digital literacy. Duration of the training varies per job role, ranging between 150 and 300 hours. Upon successful completion of their assessment, candidates shall be provided placement assistance by Training Partners (TPs). Under PMKVY, the entire training and assessment fees are paid by the Government. Payouts shall be provided to the TPs in alignment with the Common Norms. Trainings imparted under the short-term training component of the scheme shall be NSQF Level 5 and below.

**B. Recognition of Prior Learning:** Individuals with prior learning experience or skills shall be assessed and certified under the Recognition of Prior Learning (RPL) component of the scheme. RPL aims to align the competencies of the unregulated workforce of the country to the NSQF. Project Implementing Agencies (PIAs), such as Sector Skill Councils (SSCs) or any other agencies designated by MSDE/NSDC, shall be incentivized to implement RPL projects in any of the three project types (RPL Camps, RPL at Employers Premises and RPL Centres). To address knowledge gaps, PIAs may offer Bridge Courses to RPL candidates.

**6.6.2 Special Projects:** The special projects component of PMKVY envisages the creation of a platform that will facilitate trainings in special areas and/or premises of Government bodies, corporates or industry bodies, and trainings in special job roles not defined under the available Qualification Packs (QPs)/National Occupational Standards (NOSs). Special projects are projects that require some deviation from the terms and conditions of short-term training under PMKVY for any stakeholder. A proposing stakeholder can be either Government institutions of Central and State Government(s)/Autonomous Body/Statutory Body or any other equivalent body or corporates who desire to provide training to candidates.

**6.6.3 Kaushal and Rozgar Mela:** Social and community mobilisation is extremely critical for the success of PMKVY. Active participation of the community ensures transparency and accountability, and helps in leveraging the cumulative knowledge of the community for better functioning. In line with this, PMKVY assigns special importance to the involvement of the target beneficiaries through a defined mobilisation process. TPs shall conduct Kaushal and Rozgar Melas every 6 months with press/media coverage. They are also required to participate actively in National Career Service Melas and on-ground activities.

**6.6.4 Placement Guidelines:** PMKVY envisages to link the aptitude, aspiration, and knowledge of the skilled workforce it creates with employment opportunities and demands in the market. Every effort thereby needs to be made by the PMKVY TCs to provide placement opportunities to candidates, trained and certified under the Scheme. TPs shall also provide support to entrepreneurship development.

**6.6.5 Monitoring Guidelines:** To ensure that high standards of quality are maintained by TCs, NSDC and empanelled inspection agencies shall use various methodologies, such as self-audit reporting, call validations, surprise visits, and monitoring through the Skills Development Management System (SDMS). These methodologies shall be enhanced with the engagement of latest technologies.

The scheme will be implemented through the National Skill Development Corporation (NSDC).

In his speech while presenting the Budget for 2017-18 to the Parliament, late Finance Minister Mr. Arun Jaitley observed, "*Pradhan Mantri Kaushal Kendras* (PMKK) have already been promoted in more than 60 districts. We now propose to extend these *Kendras* to more than 600 districts across the country. 100 India International Skills Centres will be established across the country. These Centres would offer advanced training and also courses in foreign languages. This will help those of our youth who seek job opportunities outside the country.

In 2017-18, we also propose to launch the Skill Acquisition and Knowledge Awareness for Livelihood Promotion (SANKALP) programme at a cost of ₹ 4,000 crore. SANKALP will provide market relevant training to 3.5 crore youth.

The next phase of Skill Strengthening for Industrial Value Enhancement (STRIVE) will also be launched in 2017-18 at a cost of ₹ 2,200 crore. STRIVE will focus on improving the quality and market relevance of vocational training provided in ITIs and strengthen the apprenticeship programmes through industry cluster approach". [3]

### 6.7 Udaan

Udaan is a Special Industry Initiative for Jammu and Kashmir (J&K) in the nature of partnership between the corporates of India and Ministry of Home Affairs and implemented by National Skill Development Corporation. The programme aims to provide skills training and enhance the employability of unemployed youth of J&K. The scheme covers graduates, post-graduates and three year engineering diploma holders. It has two objectives:

1. To provide an exposure to the unemployed graduates to the best of Corporate India;
2. To provide Corporate India, an exposure to the rich talent

pool available in the State.

3. The key stakeholders are:
4. Ministry of Home Affairs (MHA): Chief Benefactors.
5. State Government (Jammu and Kashmir).
6. Corporates: Training Partners.
7. Implementation Agency: NSDC.

The scheme aims to cover 40,000 youth of J&K over a period of 5 years and a sum of ₹ 750 crore has been earmarked for implementation of the scheme over a period of 5 years to cover other incidental expenses such as travel cost, boarding and lodging, stipend and travel and medical insurance cost for the trainees and administration cost. Further corporates are eligible for partial reimbursement of training expense incurred for the candidates who have been offered jobs.

### 6.8 Skill Loan Scheme

Launched on July 15, 2015, the scheme will make available loans ranging from ₹ 5,000-₹ 1.5 lakh to 34 lakh youth of India seeking to attend skill development programmes over the next 5 years.

### 6.9 National Apprenticeship Training Scheme (NATS)

Apprenticeship is a time-tested way of learning a craft or trade under a master craftsman. Apprenticeship training is a procedure where young, technically qualified people undergo training under a master trainer to become equipped for jobs in the modern scenario. It has the double benefit of earning while learning. Apprenticeship is an agreement between a person (an apprentice) who wants to learn a skill and an employer who needs a skilled worker. The apprentices are taught the latest applications, processes and methodologies in their respective fields of work from some of the most renowned organisations in India. This also acts as a transition phase for a school/ college student from classroom to a working background. The apprentice also learns soft skills, work culture, ethics and organisational behaviour while undergoing training. This goes a long way in helping him/ her secure permanent employment in the future. At the end of training they are issued a certificate attesting to their training and proficiency in a particular field. This serves as an experience certificate when they seek employment after their training.

NATS, sponsored by Ministry of Human Resource Development, Government of India, is a one year programme equipping technically qualified youth with practical knowledge and skills required in their field of work. The apprentices are imparted training by the organizations at their place of work. Trained managers with well-developed training modules ensure that apprentices learn the job quickly and competently. During the period of apprenticeship, the apprentices are paid a stipend amount, 50 percent of which is reimbursable to the employer from Government of India. At the end of the training period the apprentices are issued a certificate of proficiency by Government of India which can be registered at all employment exchanges across India as valid employment experience. The apprentices are placed for training at Central, State and private organizations which have excellent training facilities. NATS is one of the flagship programmes of Government of India for skilling Indian youth.

### 6.10 Deen Dayal Upadhyaya Grameen Kaushalya Yojana (DDU-GKY)

The Ministry of Rural Development (MoRD), Government of India announced DDU-GKY on September 25, 2014. DDU-GKY is a part of the National Rural Livelihood Mission (NRLM), tasked with the dual objectives of adding diversity to the incomes of rural poor families and cater to the career aspirations of rural youth.

DDU-GKY is uniquely focused on rural youth between the ages of 15 and 35 years from poor families. As a part of the Skill India Campaign, it plays an instrumental role in supporting the social and economic programmes of the Government like Make in India, Digital India, Smart Cities, Start-up India, and Stand-up India campaigns.

National Policy for Skill Development and Entrepreneurship, 2015 has identified a skills gap of 109.73 million in 24 key sectors by the year 2022. This presents an unprecedented opportunity for India to train its youth population and place them in jobs across the world and realize its demographic dividend.

Innovation from partners is encouraged to build scale and capacity. Its unique implementation structure involves partners, who are by nature, committed to changing lives and are experts in their areas. They form a part of the skilling ecosystem integrated by DDU-GKY. Partners are supported through investment, capacity building, strategies for retention, linkages to international placement and technology support for training purposes.

**Endnotes**

1. Government of India, Ministry of Skill Development and Entrepreneurship, *National Skill Development Mission: A Framework for Implementation*, 2015, p. 2.
2. NPSDE, 2015 has been explained in chapter 5 of this book.
3. Government of India, Ministry of Finance, Budget Papers 2017-18, *Speech of the Finance Minister*, paras 54 to 56.

# 7

# Ministry of Skill Development and Entrepreneurship (MSDE)

Government has set up the Ministry of Skill Development and Entrepreneurship (MSDE), with an enabling framework to facilitate job creation and entrepreneurship, as well as attract private investment. Steps are also being taken to attract foreign direct investment and catapult manufacturing growth. The *Pradhan Mantri Kaushal Vikas Yojana* (Skill India Mission) is MSDE's flagship scheme to enable young Indians to take up industry-relevant skills training and improve their employability.

India presently faces a dual challenge of paucity of highly trained workforce, as well as non-employability of large sections of the conventionally educated youth, who possess little or no job skills. Ministry for Skill Development and Entrepreneurship (earlier Department of Skill Development and Entrepreneurship notified in July 2014) was set up in November 2014 to give fresh impetus to the Skill India agenda and help create an appropriate ecosystem that facilitates imparting employable skills to its growing workforce over the next few decades. Apart from meeting its own demand, India has the potential to provide skilled workforce to fill the expected shortfall in the ageing developed world.

## 7.1 Functions of MSDE

MSDE is responsible for co-ordination of all skill development efforts across the country, removal of disconnect between demand and supply of skilled manpower, building the vocational and technical training framework, skill up-gradation, building of new skills, and innovative thinking not only for existing jobs but also jobs that are to be created. MSDE aims to achieve its vision of a Skilled India. It is aided in these initiatives by its following functional arms:

1. National Skill Development Corporation (NSDC).
2. National Skill Development Fund (NSDF).
3. National Skill Development Agency (NSDA).

There are 33 sector skill councils (SSCs) as well as 187 training partners registered with NSDC. [1] The Ministry also works with the existing network of skill development centres, universities and other alliances in the field. Further, it collaborates with relevant Central Ministries, State Governments, international organizations, industry and NGOs for multi-level engagement and more impactful implementation of skill development efforts.

MSDE has been allocated following business:

1. Co-ordination with all concerned for evolving an appropriate skill development framework, removal of disconnect between the demand for and supply of skilled manpower through vocational and technical training, skill up-gradation, building of new skills, innovative thinking and talents not only for the existing jobs but also the jobs that are to be created.
2. Mapping of existing skills and their certification.
3. Expansion of youth entrepreneurship education and capacity through forging strong partnership between educational institutions, business and other community organizations and set national standards for it.
4. Role of co-ordination relating to skill development.
5. Doing market research and devising training curriculum in important sectors.
6. Industry-Institute linkages.
7. Bringing public-private-partnership (PPP) element in this activity—partnership with the industries which need the skilled manpower.
8. Making broad policies for all other Ministries/Departments with regard to market requirements and skill development.
9. Framing policies for soft skills.
10. Skill development related to information technology (IT) and computer education.

11. Academic equivalence of skill sets.
12. Skilling for entrepreneurship development for science and technology.
13. Work relating to Industrial Training Institutes (ITIs).
14. National Skill Development Corporation.
15. National Skill Development Agency.
16. National Skill Development Fund.
17. National Institute for Entrepreneurship and Small Business Development, NOIDA.
18. Indian Institute of Entrepreneurship, Guwahati.

## 7.2 National Skill Development Corporation (NSDC)

The first National Policy on Skill Development was notified in 2009. In the aftermath of this policy, National Skill Development Corporation (NSDC) was established in 2009 to promote private sector participation via innovative funding models. NSDC has tied up with more than 211 training providers, many of whom have started scaling up their operations, to offer short term training programmes. They also supported and incubated 37 sector skills councils (SSCs) which are intended to facilitate much needed participation and ownership of industry to ensure needs based training programmes.

NSDC is a public-private-partnership (PPP) initiative in India. It aims to promote skill development by catalyzing creation of large, quality, for-profit vocational institutions. NSDC provides funding to build scalable, for-profit vocational training initiatives. Its mandate is to enable support systems such as quality assurance, information systems and train the trainer academies either directly or through partnerships. NSDC acts as a catalyst in skill development by providing funding to enterprises, companies and organisations that provide skill training. It also develops appropriate models to enhance, support and coordinate private sector initiatives. The differentiated focus for the 21 sectors under NSDC's purview and its understanding of their viability makes every sector attractive to private investment.

NSDC is a not-for-profit company set up by the Ministry of Finance, under Section 25 of the Companies Act. It has an equity base of ₹ 10 crore, of which the Government of India holds 49 percent, while the private sector has the balance 51 percent.

NSDC has a two-tier structure, viz. a 15 member board and a National Skill Development Fund (NSDF) as a 100 percent Government-owned trust to facilitate its mandate of coordinating and stimulating private sector initiative in the area of skill development with enhanced flexibility and effectiveness.

**7.2.1 Vision:** NSDC was set up as part of a national skill development mission to fulfil the growing need in India for skilled manpower across sectors and narrow the existing gap between the demand and supply of skills. The Union Finance Minister announced the formation of the National Skill Development Corporation (NSDC) in his Budget Speech (2008-09): "There is a compelling need to launch a world-class skill development programme in a mission mode that will address the challenge of imparting the skills required by a growing economy. Both the structure and the leadership of the mission must be such that the programme can be scaled up quickly to cover the whole country".

**7.2.2 Mission:**

1. Upgrade skills to international standards through significant industry involvement and develop necessary frameworks for standards, curriculum and quality assurance.
2. Enhance, support and co-ordinate private sector initiatives for skill development through appropriate public-private-partnership (PPP) models; and strive for significant operational and financial involvement from the private sector.
3. Play the role of a *market-maker* by bringing financing, particularly in sectors where market mechanisms are ineffective or missing.

4. Prioritize initiatives that can have a multiplier or catalytic effect as opposed to one-off impact.

**7.2.3 Objective:** NSDC was formed to achieve the target of skilling/up-skilling 150 million people by 2022 by fostering private sector initiatives in the skill development space. NSDC along with the support of its 31 sector skill councils and 136 training partners works continuously in collaboration with each other, to create a successful model for the country which is being evaluated periodically for improvement and effectiveness.

To ensure superior decision-making, the NSDC requires a structure and governance model that provides it with autonomy, stature and continuity. Thus, the organisation has a tiered decision-making structure:

**7.2.4 Functions:** NSDC plays three key roles:

1. **Funding and Incentivising**: In the near term this is a key role. This involves providing financing either as loans or equity, providing grants and supporting financial incentives to select private sector initiatives to improve financial viability through tax breaks etc. The exact nature of funding (equity, loan and grant) depends on the viability or attractiveness of the segment and, to some extent, the type of player (for-profit private, non-profit industry association or non-profit NGO). Over time, the NSDC aspires to create strong viable business models and reduce its grant-making role.
2. **Enabling Support Services**: A skills development institute requires a number of inputs or support services such as curriculum, faculty and their training, standards and quality assurance, technology platforms, student placement mechanisms and so on. The NSDC plays a significant enabling role in some of these support services, most importantly and in the near-term, setting up standards and accreditation systems in partnership with industry associations.
3. **Shaping/Creating**: In the near-term, the NSDC proactively

provides momentum for large-scale participation by private players in skill development. NSDC identifies critical skill groups, develops models for skill development and attracts potential private players and provides support to these efforts.

**7.2.5 Advocacy and Communications:** NSDC has a robust communications strategy to keep the momentum of the programme going and also encourage young people to come forward and get skilled. There is constant creation of content and marketing material (poster campaign, STAR animation video, TVC's etc.) which is available with NSDC which the partners and all other stakeholders can use to talk about their skilling programme.

NSDC launched its advertisement campaign *Hunar Hai to Kadar Hai* with two television commercials which aired in February-March 2014. These TVCs talked about the success stories of real people with real ambitions in the automotive and retail sector, and are available for marketing purpose.

A helpline number 088000-55555 which was announced during the TVC, link potential trainees with the nearby training centres and educate them about the offerings of the programme. NSDC is also actively engaging with all its stakeholder holders on social media platform.

**7.2.6 Innovation and Engagement Units:** The innovation and engagement practice within NSDC has two key focus areas. The innovation unit is focused on supporting high impact and innovative solutions that can disrupt the skilling ecosystem and/or enhance outcomes manifold, preferably in sectors and regions with unmet needs. The engagement unit works with both internal and external stakeholders to strengthen the skills ecosystem, thus contributing to the larger NSDC mission.

**A. Innovation Unit:** In the effort to meet the incremental demands in vocational skills, evaluate past efforts and generate new ideas, this unit looks at sustainable ideas that can add value to the vocational training ecosystem across various categories under the larger skills framework. Based on the understanding of the ecosystem, the following 4 key areas have been identified for support:

1. Sourcing and financing.
2. Training to certification.
3. Placement and linkages.
4. Post-placement support.

**B. Engagement Unit:** The activities of the engagement unit can broadly be classified as below:

1. **Assistance:** The team works with partners that are under-performing to assist them in strengthening their business plans through deep dive analysis and external support through a select group of turnaround specialists. It also carries out business restructuring in cases where there is continuous under- performance and the initial plan targets might not be met during the term period.
2. **External Engagement:** The team works with multiple stakeholders including corporates, foundations, corporate social responsibility (CSR) arms, impact funds, incubators, market facilitators etc. to design and support high impact collaborative projects to enhance skilling outcomes, thus achieving multiplier effect.

**7.2.7 Corporate Social Responsibility (CSR) for Skill Development:** NSDC works with corporates, foundations, government, and community-based organizations in structuring high impact collaborative projects.

The Companies Act, 2013, which came into effect on April 1, 2014, lists corporate social responsibility (CSR) mandate for Indian companies.

The 2013 Act makes an effort to introduce the culture of corporate social responsibility (CSR) in Indian corporates by requiring companies to formulate a corporate social responsibility policy and at least incur a given minimum expenditure on social activities.

It may be recalled that the Ministry of Corporate Affairs (MCA) had introduced the Corporate Social Responsibility Voluntary Guidelines in 2009. These guidelines have now been incorporated within the 2013 Act and have obtained legal sanctity. Section 135 of the 2013 Act, seeks to provide that every company having a net worth of ₹ 500 crore, or more or a turnover of ₹ 1,000 crore or more, or a net profit of ₹ 5 crore or more, during any financial year shall constitute the corporate social responsibility committee of the board. This committee needs to comprise of three or more directors, out of which, at least one director should be an independent director. The composition of the committee shall be included in the board's report. The committee shall formulate the policy, including activities specified in Schedule VII, which are as follows:

1. Eradicating extreme hunger and poverty.
2. Promotion of education.
3. Promoting gender equality and empowering women.
4. Reducing child mortality and improving maternal health.
5. Combating human immunodeficiency virus, acquired immune deficiency syndrome, malaria and other diseases.
6. Ensuring environmental sustainability.
7. Employment enhancing vocational skills.
8. Social business projects.
9. Contribution to the Prime Minister's National Relief Fund or any other fund set-up by the central government or the state governments for socio-economic development and relief, and funds for the welfare of the scheduled castes and tribes, other backward classes, minorities and women.
10. Such other matters as may be prescribed.

There have been mixed reactions to the introduction of the 'spend or explain' approach taken by the MCA with respect to CSR. It may take a while before all of Corporate India imbibes CSR as a culture.

However, activities specified in the Schedule are not elaborate or detailed enough to indicate the kind of projects that could be undertaken, for example, environment sustainability or social business projects could encompass a wide range of activities.

The committee will also need to recommend the amount of

expenditure to be incurred and monitor the policy from time-to-time. The board shall disclose the contents of the policy in its report, and place it on the website, if any, of the company. The 2013 Act mandates that these companies would be required to spend at least 2 percent of the average net profits of the immediately preceding three years on CSR activities, and if not spent, explanation for the reasons thereof would need to be given in the director's report (Section 135 of the 2013 Act).

NSDC has evolved a robust framework to solicit funds for skill development projects in line with these guidelines. NSDC can assist any entity to design structure and manage skill development projects due to its nation-wide presence through its training organizations.

Project can be structured through a direct bipartite agreement, or a tripartite agreement with contributions to the National Skill Development Fund, a Government of India fund under Ministry of Skill Development and Entrepreneurship. All projects are implemented through approved training partners of NSDC, with monitoring and reporting of project outcomes provided centrally by NSDC. NSDC actively participates in CSR discussions to advocate for skill development through outreach events, industry forums, one-on-one consultations and other ways.

## 7.3 National Skill Development Fund (NSDF)

Skill development brings return to the individual, the employing enterprise and the economy as a whole. Therefore, all stakeholders—Government, both at Centre and States, public and private enterprises, and the direct beneficiary, i.e. the individual—should share the burden of mobilizing financial or in-kind resources for skill development.

NSDF, operating arm of the NSDC, was created in 2009 with a corpus of ₹ 995.10 crore as Government-owned trust to receive financial contributions from donors, private entities, governments (both Central and State), statutory bodies, financial institutions etc. NSDC and NSDF would enter into an investment management agreement whereby NSDF would provide funds to NSDC for furtherance of the objective of skill development in accordance with the approved work and financial plan. NSDC would charge a management fee from NSDF for managing its resources. The beneficiaries of the trust are the youth of India who require skill development and vocational training. Its main functions are as follows:

1. Making periodic as well as an annual report of its plans and activities and put them in the public domain.
2. Establishing a trainee placement and tracking system for effective evaluation and future policy planning.
3. Establishing credible independent certification systems for both vocational education (VE) and vocational training (VT) with the scope for permitting vertical and horizontal mobility within and between VE and VT.

The Fund is contributed by various Government sources, and other donors/contributors to enhance, stimulate and develop the skills of Indian youth by various sector-specific programmes. A public trust, set up by the Government of India, is the custodian of the Fund. The Trust accepts donations, contributions in cash or kind from the contributors for furtherance of objectives of the Fund. The Fund is operated and managed by the board of trustees. The chief executive officer of the trust is responsible for day-to-day administration and management of the Trust.

Accounts of the trust are subject to CAG Audit and are also audited by a Chartered Accountant for every financial year and in such manner as may be directed by Government of India. The Trust has engaged IL&FS Trust Company Ltd. (ITCL), one of the largest corporate trustees in India, for providing micro prudential oversight on the implementing partner and monitoring the interests of Trust.

The Fund meets its objectives through National Skill Development Corporation (NSDC) which is an industry-led not-for-profit-company set up for building skill development capacity and forging strong linkages with the market. NSDC acts as a catalyst in skill development by providing funding to enterprises, companies and organizations that provide skill training. It also develops appropriate models to enhance, support and coordinate private sector initiatives. Till March 31, 2015, NSDF had released ₹ 2,333 crore to NSDC towards skill development programmes including National Skill Certification and Monetary Reward Scheme (STAR) and UDAAN Scheme (J&K-oriented). NSDC with 160 training partners and 1,722 training centres has so far trained around 35 lakh persons across India.

## 7.4 National Skill Development Agency (NSDA)

NSDA was notified through a gazette notification dated June 6, 2013. NSDA is an autonomous body (registered as a society under the Societies Registration Act, 1860) of Ministry of Skill Development and Entrepreneurship, which coordinates and harmonizes the skill development efforts of the Government and the private sector to achieve the skilling targets. It endeavours to bridge the social, regional, gender and economic divide through the following:

1. By ensuring that the skilling needs of the disadvantaged and marginalized groups like SCs, STs, OBCs, minorities, women and differently-abled persons are taken care of through the various skill development programmes.
2. By taking affirmative actions as part of advocacy by the NSDA. NSDA anchors the National Skills Qualifications Framework (NSQF) and facilitates the setting up of professional certifying bodies in addition to the existing ones.

**7.4.1 Functions:** NSDA discharges the following functions:

1. Take all possible steps to meet skilling targets as envisaged in the Twelfth Five Year Plan (2012-17) and beyond.
2. Co-ordinate and harmonize the approach to skill development among various Central Ministries/Departments, State Governments, NSDC and the private sector.
3. Anchor and operationalize the NSQF to ensure that quality and standards meet sector-specific requirements.

4. Be the nodal agency for state skill development missions.
5. Raise extra-budgetary resources for skill development from various sources such as international agencies, including multilateral agencies, and the private sector.
6. Evaluate existing skill development schemes with a view to assessing their efficacy and suggest corrective action to make them more effective.
7. Create and maintain a national data base related to skill development including development of a dynamic labour market information system (LMIS).
8. Take affirmative action for advocacy.
9. Ensure that the skilling needs of the disadvantaged and the marginalized groups like SCs, STs, OBCs, minorities, women and differently-abled persons are taken care of.
10. Discharge any other function as may be assigned to it by the Government of India.

**7.4.2 Other Activities:**

**A. Rationalization of the Skill Development Schemes of the Government of India:** NSDA has worked with the concerned ministries and stakeholders to achieve convergence of norms across the various central schemes for skill development, while at the same time recognizing the special needs of the North-Eastern States, the hill States, and other geographies that pose challenging situations for skill development.

**B. Creation of an Integrated Labour Market Information System:** A national database on all major aspects of skill development has been created in partnership with all other Ministries of the Government of India and the State Governments. This is a one-shop stop where all the relevant information is freely available to citizens. The government has created a National Steering Committee for setting up the Labour Market Information System (LMIS). The LMIS would bring in operational efficiencies, would be transparent and available to all, and would help reduce considerably the situation of one individual being benefited under different schemes.

**C. Engagement with States:** NSDA is actively engaged

with various State Governments to plan out their skill development action plans, help them develop their skill development policies, and set up suitable administrative mechanisms. Through Technical Assistance Programmes with the Asian Development bank (ADB), European Union (EU) and Department for International Development (DFID) of the Government of UK, NSDA is helping the State Skill Development Missions of various states to build their respective capacities.

**D. Skills Innovation Initiative:** A committee has been set up under the Skills Innovation Initiative housed under the NSDA. NSDA invites innovative ideas, concepts and practices on skill development. The Committee reviews all the proposals of innovations to facilitate their application on a wider scale. Selected innovative practices are facilitated and propagated for wider application.

### 7.5 MoU between MSDE and Ministry of Health and Family Welfare (MHFW) on Skill Development

MSDE signed on July 11, 2015 a MoU with MHFW to establish a framework for concerted and comprehensive joint action to address the need for skilled human resources in the health sector. Besides achieving the national goals of skilling youth so as to increase their employability, the MoU also seeks to upgrade the quality and reach of human and infrastructural resources that is at the core of a quality healthcare system.

Some of the significant outcomes of the MoU are as under:

1. Significantly increase the present capacities in areas of health sector to a minimum of 1 lakh trainees.
2. Make significant savings of public resources by way of leveraging the existing infrastructure of government and private sector healthcare institutions to provide training against various short-term job roles.
3. Explore pooling of financial resources of the two departments and allow for international partnerships to provide greater financial muscle to the programme.

4. Create a framework of certification by Health Sector Skill Council of select job roles and for absorption of the trainees in the health sector.
5. Create a framework for recognition of prior learning.
6. Allow for seamless vertical and horizontal mobility of trainees at various levels of skill development.

## 7.6 MoU between MSDE and Ministry of Steel and Mines (MSM) on Skill Development

MSDE and MSM signed on July 10, 2015 a MoU on skill development. The MoU was signed with an understanding to collectively address the incremental human resource requirement in the two sectors. MSDE will implement this partnership through Directorate General of Training (DGT) and National Skill Development Corporation (NSDC).

The two Ministries will together ensure standardized vocational training and infrastructure for the industry so that it becomes a self-sufficient and progressive industry and also creates more opportunities globally.

## 7.7 Other Ministries Related to Skill Development

**7.7.1 Ministry of Human Resource Development (MHRD):** MHRD was created on September 26, 1985. Currently, the MHRD works through two departments:

1. Department of School Education and Literacy.
2. Department of Higher Education.

Department of School Education and Literacy is responsible for development of school education and literacy in the country. It has its eyes set on the *universalisation of education* and making better citizens out of India's young brigade. For this, various new schemes and initiatives are taken up regularly and recently, those schemes and initiatives have also started paying dividends in the form of growing enrolment in schools.

Department of Higher Education takes care of what is one of the largest higher education systems of the world, just after the United States and China. It is engaged in bringing world class opportunities of higher education and research to the country so that Indian students are not found lacking when facing an international platform. For this, the Government has launched joint ventures and signed MoUs to help the Indian students benefit from the world opinion.

The main objectives of MHRD are as under:

1. Formulating the national policy on education and to ensure that it is implemented in letter and spirit.
2. Planned development, including expanding access and improving quality of the educational institutions throughout the country, including the regions where people do not have easy access to education.
3. Paying special attention to disadvantaged groups like the poor, females and the minorities.
4. Provide financial help in the form of scholarships, loan subsidy etc. to deserving students from deprived sections of the society.
5. Encouraging international co-operation in the field of education, including working closely with the UNESCO and foreign governments as well as universities, to enhance the educational opportunities in the country.

**7.7.2 Ministry of Labour and Employment:** Ministry of Labour and Employment is one of the oldest and important Ministries of the Government of India. The main responsibility of the Ministry is to protect and safeguard the interests of workers in general and the poor, deprived and disadvantaged sections of the society, in particular. Further it aims to creating a healthy work environment for higher production and productivity and to develop and coordinate vocational skill training and employment.

The vision of the Ministry is: (a) to provide decent working conditions and improved quality of life of workers, (b) ensuring India without child labour in hazardous sectors and (c) enhancing employability through employment services and skill development on a sustainable basis.

Its mission is: (a) improving the working conditions and the quality of life of workers through laying down and implementing policies, programmes, schemes and projects for providing social security and welfare measures, (b) regulating conditions of work, occupational health and safety of workers, (c) eliminating child labour from hazardous occupations and processes, (d) strengthening enforcement of labour laws and (e) promoting skill development and employment services.

At present, there are 44 labour related statutes enacted by the Central Government dealing with minimum wages, accidental and social security benefits, occupational safety and health, conditions of employment, disciplinary action, formation of trade unions, industrial relations, etc. Government's attention is also focused on promotion of welfare and providing social security to the labour force both in organized and unorganized sectors, in tandem with the process of liberalization. These objectives are sought to be achieved through implementation of various labour laws, which regulate the terms and conditions of service and employment of workers. The State Governments are also empowered to enact legislations, as labour is a subject in the concurrent list under the Constitution of India.

To sum up, skills and knowledge are driving forces of economic growth and social development for any country. Countries with higher levels and better standards of skills adjust more effectively to the challenges and opportunities in domestic and international job markets. For a skills strategy to be successful, it should be complemented by commensurate creation of jobs in the primary, secondary and tertiary sectors.

As India moves progressively towards becoming a global knowledge economy, it must meet the rising aspirations of its youth. This can be partially achieved through focus on advancement of skills that are relevant to the emerging economic environment. The challenge pertains not only to a huge quantitative expansion of the facilities for skill training, but also to the equally important task of raising their quality.

Skill development, however, cannot be viewed in

isolation. Skills are germane to, but not always sufficient for securing adequate economic dividends. Skills need to be an integral part of employment and economic growth strategies to spur employability and productivity. Coordination with other national macroeconomic paradigms and growth strategies is therefore critical.

Skill development programmes of the Central Government over the years have been spread across more than 20 Ministries/Departments without any robust coordination and monitoring mechanism to ensure convergence. The scenario is no different in most of the states except the few states which have moved towards functional convergence by creating State Missions. This legacy has resulted in multiplicity of norms, procedures, curricula, certifications etc. Further, many of these skill development initiatives often remain unaligned to demand, thus defeating its entire objective.

Productive and formal employment generation depends on the availability of an adequately skilled labour force through sustained investments in skills development and fostering opportunities for decent job creation through entrepreneurship. To close India's skills deficit and increase employability, a range of policies and strategies are needed to address work-relevant education systems, career guidance, life-skills, and technical, vocational education and training schemes, along with on-the-job training in both formal and informal sectors.

**Endnote**

1. Sector Skill Councils (SSCs) are set up as autonomous industry-led bodies by NSDC. They create occupational standards and qualification bodies, develop competency framework, conduct train-the-trainer programmes, conduct skill gap studies and assess and certify trainees on the curriculum aligned to national occupational standards developed by them.

# 8

# Areas of Concern and Future Challenges

Although India has the advantage of a large pool of human resources, the industry continues to face deficit in manpower possessing the right skills for manufacturing, service, marketing etc. State level institutions such as district industries centres (DICs), which could play an important role in capacity building, have been unable to transform themselves from regulating bodies to facilitating agencies. Their current infrastructure is sub-optimally utilised.

The development of the small-scale sector has been hampered due to the shortage of trained and experienced managerial and supervisory personnel. Provision of technical services is needed to stimulate productive efficiency and new product lines. Most MSMEs do not have money to invest in market research and are unable to carry out design and technical improvements to keep up with market demands. Unlike big businesses, they cannot invest in advertising and packaging. This limits their ability to tap markets and attract consumers. MSMEs, especially those pertaining to traditional livelihoods are, therefore, increasingly being forced to rely on middle men, petty traders and big businesses to market their products.

Lack of skilled manpower and information as well as lack of reach to modern technology are key issues affecting the growth of MSME sector. It is often said that India enjoys a *demographic dividend* compared to rest of the world due to its huge population in productive age group. Most of the other developed as well as developing countries face the threat of an aging population. If this comparative advantage can be augmented with adequate skill development, India can become the global supplier of quality manpower. In this backdrop, the

Government has decided to accord top priority to skill development.

**8.1 Technology Upgradation and Support**

Technology development calls for both general and specific forms of human capital, and emerging technologies are highly skill intensive in both technical and managerial terms. While India is endowed at present with large amounts of high-level human capital, investments in the creation of new skills (as measured by enrolment levels in technical subjects at all levels) are low. In addition, firm level investments in training are highly variable, and large parts of industry invest very little in training. The small and medium enterprises (SMEs) sector in particular suffers from very low levels of skill, while industrial training institutes are often unresponsive to their needs.

R&D in Indian industry has been rising, but the overall level is still low and over three-quarters of research effort originates in the public sector. This is in contrast to Taiwan and Korea, where most of R&D is undertaken by industrial enterprises. It is important for the Government to analyse current technological trends in industry in order to formulate appropriate policies to encourage R&D.

Technology upgrading requires that Indian enterprises of all types have information on relevant technologies in international markets and also within the country. Many countries have well-developed systems of computerised on-line technology information and dissemination services, often backed up with consultancy and financial assistance for small and medium enterprises to enable them to know about, test, and implement new technologies. The availability of similar facilities is weak in India. Note needs to be taken of the emerging trends of restrictions on access to technology through stringent intellectual property restrictions and on dual use technologies by certain groups of industrially advanced countries. Special efforts have to be made, both at national as well as at international levels, to ensure that such restrictions do not inhibit progress in high technology sectors.

India has a large infrastructure of technology support institutions, some of which are undergoing reform to make them more relevant to industrial needs. A number of universities, especially the IITs, are interacting increasingly with industry on technological matters, while others are outside this circle. There is a need to strengthen technology foresight programmes to analyse the implications of emerging technologies, analyse domestic strengths and weaknesses and target future technologies for local development.

Technology development generally requires the setting up of clusters of industries that can share information and skills, as in *science parks* or dedicated industrial estates. Some such facilities exist in India, but their efficacy and functioning need to be strengthened.

### 8.2 Labour Market Information System (LMIS)

In this context the Twelfth Five Year Plan (2012-17) remarked, "Currently, there is no common platform where industry, job seekers and government can share information and take informed decisions. Prospective employees may acquire skills which have little or no demand or may take a career path which has little relevance in the market. The government does not have reliable data source of industry demand/available skills and the labour market conditions with the result effective policy decisions impacting training and enhancing employment potential of youth cannot be taken. This situation is disappointing for both prospective employers and employees resulting in job mismatch and low and inferior quality output.

This necessitates the implementation of a labour market information system (LMIS) which would pave the way for a shared platform providing quantitative and qualitative information and intelligence on the labour market to all the stakeholders for making informed plans, choices, and decisions related to their business requirements, career planning, education and training programmes, job search, recruitment, labour policies and workforce investment strategies. LMIS would facilitate formulation of effective policies for filling the skills gap; evaluating results of labour related policies and programmes; providing key indicators on demand and supply labour. It would assist the job seekers take informed decisions about their future career development by providing information on the needs of the labour market; identify current and future job market opportunities; provide analysis of the labour market based on the economic development and also enable employers take decisions about upgrading their employees' skills; access information on skills available in the labour market; different labour characteristics such as labour policies, labour costs and so on". [1]

## 8.3 Quality and Relevance of Skill Development

Quality and relevance of skill development are keys to India's global competitiveness as well as improving an individual's access to decent employment. For enterprises to compete in the global economy, the quality of training must reach world standards and be relevant to the needs of national and international markets.

To increase the relevance with future employment market including promotion of self-employment, soft skills and entrepreneurship skills need to be made integral part of skill development. The demographic advantage that the country enjoys, coupled with prospects of global shortages in skills as the world population ages, means that the country could be supplying skills to the world.

Quality assurance is based on the following 5 key functions:

1. Validation of qualifications for ensuring that qualifications reflect market needs and workplace requirements and are expressed in the form of competencies with clear assessment criteria.
2. Validation of training process for ensuring that proper tools,

techniques, methodologies and material, as suggested in the curriculum/standards are used by the resource persons.

3. Quality assured assessment of learners for ensuring that assessment is based on national standards (competencies) and uses valid and reliable assessment methods.
4. Accreditation of training providers and training institutions for ensuring that training is delivered by competent and qualified trainers in well-resourced and managed institutions.
5. Research and information for linking the supply of skilled workers to trends in well-researched labour market information (LMI) covering both the organised and unorganised sectors of the economy.

The objective of enforcing quality and relevance in skill development can be realized through improvement in infrastructure, quality of trainer and development of National Vocational Qualification Framework.

**8.3.1 Quality of Infrastructure:** It can be ensured by following measures:

1. Extensive use of information and communication technology (ICT) for learning or increasing the impact of learning.
2. Optimum use of existing physical infrastructure in multiple shifts or otherwise.
3. Industries should provide their spare capacity to supplement skill development activities.
4. Physical infrastructure should be created, expanded and upgraded according to skill requirement of specific sectors of economy.

**8.3.2 Quality of Trainer:** It needs following initiatives:

1. Innovative ways of recruiting trainers, including the employment of former trainees who have gained workplace experience and of practitioners of a craft, trained as master craft persons.
2. Innovative skill development schemes in which trainees acquire theoretical learning at the institution while

obtaining practical skills in the workplace.

3. Retired employees, mainly from defence forces, should be retrained to meet the requirement of trainers.
4. Award and incentive mechanisms, including reward and career progression systems, should be reviewed and institutionalized to improve the status of trainers.
5. Special efforts to improve the gender balance among trainers.

## 8.4 Skill Development and Demographic Dividend Hypothesis

There is a thinking that if the massive population of India is properly educated and trained, it can prove a boon for the national economy. India's demographic dividend is essentially due to two factors: (a) declining birth rates and (b) improvement in life expectancy. The declining birth rate changes the age distribution and makes for a smaller proportion of population in the dependent ages and for relatively larger share in the productive labour force. The result is low dependency ratio which can provide comparative cost advantage and competitiveness to the economy. Moreover, the global economy is expected to witness a skilled man power shortage to the extent of around 56 million by 2020. Thus, the *demographic dividend* in India needs to be exploited not only to expand the production possibility frontier but also to meet the skilled manpower requirements of India and other countries. [2]

Sounding a note of optimism on demographic trends in India, the Approach Paper to the Eleventh Five Year Plan (2007-12) remarked, "In the longer run, there is another important potential strength arising from our demographic trends. Our dependency rate (ratio of dependent to working age population) is falling whereas that of industrialised countries and even China is rising. The presence of a skilled young population in an environment where investment is expanding and the industrial world ageing could be a major advantage. It is, however, important to realise that we can only reap this demographic dividend if we invest massively on human resource development and skill formation and create an economic environment capable of absorbing our relatively young working population in productive employment". [3]

To reap the benefits of *demographic dividend*, the Eleventh Five Year Plan (2007-2012) had favoured the creation of a comprehensive National Skill Development Mission. As a result, a Coordinated Action on Skill Development with three-tier institutional structure consisting of: (a) Prime Minister's National Council on Skill Development (NCSD), (b) National Skill Development Coordination Board (NSDCB) and (c) National Skill Development Corporation (NSDC) was created in early 2008.

Whereas NSDC has spelt out policy advice, and direction in the form of *core principles* and has given a Vision to create 500 million skilled people by 2022 through skill systems (which must have high degree of inclusivity), NSDCB has taken upon itself the task of coordinating the skill development efforts of a large number of Central Ministries/Departments and States. The NSDC has geared itself for preparing comprehensive action plans and activities which would promote public-private-partnership (PPP) models of financing skill development.

The three-tier structure has laid the institutional foundations for a more proactive role of public (Centre plus States) and private and third sector interactions and interfaces for harnessing the benefits of demographic dividend. It has also been able to focus on skill development through the creation of a coordinating mechanism. It has also made the issue of skill development as an important agenda for Central and State Governments.

**8.4.1 Twelfth Five Year Plan (2012-17) on Demographic Dividend:** Stipulating the conditions for reaping the demographic dividend, the Approach Paper to Twelfth Plan remarked, "India has a younger population not only in comparison to advanced economies but also in relation to the large developing countries. As a result, the labour force in India is expected to increase by 32 percent over the next 20 years, while it will decline by 4 percent in industrialised countries and by nearly 5 percent in China. This demographic dividend can add to growth potential, provided two conditions are fulfilled. First, higher levels of health, education and skill development must be achieved. Second, an environment must be created in which the economy not only grows rapidly, but also enhances good quality employment/livelihood opportunities to meet the needs and aspirations of the youth. [4]

It was earlier assumed that population growth during demographic transition will lead to overcrowding, poverty, under-nutrition, environmental deterioration, poor quality of life and increase in disease burden. Experience in the last few decades has shown that this may not always be correct. India is currently in the phase of demographic transition when the increase in population is mainly among younger, better educated and healthy population with low morbidity and mortality rate. The challenge for the health sector is to promote healthy life styles, improve access to and utilisation of healthcare so that the country can achieve substantial reduction in mortality and morbidity.

Occupational health and environmental health programmes need be augmented to ensure that working population remain healthy and productive. If these challenges are fully met, it is possible to accelerate reduction in morbidity and mortality rate in this age group and improve health indices of the country.

With growing number of senior citizens there may be substantial increase in healthcare needs especially for management of non-communicable diseases. Increasing availability and awareness about technological advances for management of these problems, rising expectations of the population and the ever-escalating cost of healthcare are some of the problems that the healthcare system has to cope with. Healthcare delivery systems will have to gear up to taking up necessary preventive, promotive, curative and rehabilitative care for growing population of senior citizens.

### 8.5 Future Challenges

As the proportion of working age group of 15-59 years will be increasing steadily, India has the advantage of *demographic dividend.* Harnessing the demographic dividend through appropriate skill development efforts would provide an opportunity to achieve inclusion and productivity within the country and also a reduction in the global skill shortages. Large scale skill development is thus an imminent imperative.

Major challenge of skill development initiatives is also to address the needs of huge population by providing skills in order to make them employable and help them secure *decent work.* Skill development for persons working in the unorganized sector is a key strategy in that direction. This will also inculcate dignity of labour and create greater awareness towards environmental, safety and health concerns.

Planned development of skills must be underpinned by a policy which is both comprehensive as well as national in character. A national policy response is, therefore, needed to guide the skill development strategies and coordinated action by all stakeholders to avoid a piecemeal approach. It is also important that the policies of skill development be linked to policies in the economic, employment and social development arenas.

The country is poised at a moment in history when a much brighter future for its entire people is within its reach. Skill development will help actualize this potential. Development and articulation of a national policy on skill development is a matter of priority. A task of skill development has many challenges which include, inter alia, the following:

1. Increasing capacity and capability of existing system to ensure equitable access to all.
2. Promoting life-long learning, maintaining quality and relevance, according to changing requirement, particularly of emerging knowledge economy.
3. Creating effective convergence between school education, various skill development efforts of government and between

government and private sector initiative.

4. Capacity building of institutions for planning, quality assurance and involvement of stake holders.
5. Creating institutional mechanism for research and development, quality assurance, examinations and certification, affiliations and accreditation.
6. Increasing participation of stakeholders, mobilizing adequate investment for financing skill development, attaining sustainability by strengthening physical and intellectual resources.

The country, however, has a big challenge ahead as it is estimated that only 4.69 percent of the total workforce in India has undergone formal skill training as compared to 68 percent in UK, 75 percent in Germany, 52 percent in USA, 80 percent in Japan and 96 percent in South Korea. While the debate on the exact quantum of the challenge continues, there is no disputing the fact that it is indeed a challenge of 5 formidable proportion.

One of the major challenges in the country today is public perception on skilling, which is viewed as the last option meant for those who have not been able to progress in the formal academic system. A number of factors are responsible for this state of affairs:

1. Social and traditional view that sees status as being inversely proportional to the degree to which one works with one's hands. This can also be attributed to primeval and archaic ethos which compartmentalized the skilling landscape for several hundred years. This unfortunate legacy has no moral, ethical and constitutional sanction in free India. Nonetheless, this gets at times manifested in norms, attitudes and societal behaviour.
2. The proclivity of large sections of industry especially in the micro, small and medium sectors to treat skilled and unskilled persons at par, thereby depriving skilling of any meaningful economic incentive.
3. Most of the vocational training programmes are not

aligned to the requirements of the industry As a result of the above, a piquant situation exists in the country wherein unemployment continues to coexist with lack of requisite number of skilled people at functional level to build roads and bridges, lay pipelines, work in factories, engage in offshore drilling, build ships etc.

Different states in India face varied challenges in relation to demographics and skill development. There needs to be a shared sense of urgency to address the challenges of the changing demography. While State Skill Development Missions (SSDMs) have been launched in almost all States, there is an imminent need for capacity building and empowerment of SSDMs in many States in order to upscale quality skill development.

The various grant-based, free training programmes available today, though necessary, have their own limitations especially on quality and employability. Students undergoing training for free attach little value to training whereas training providers focus on increasing their numbers rather than quality of training. While financial support is required for certain industry sectors or segments of unorganised sector, it is critical to exercise utmost discretion and link employability with all such efforts.

There is multiplicity in assessment and certification systems existing in the country which leads to inconsistent outcomes and causes confusion to the employers. The availability of good quality trainers is a major area of concern. There is a lack of focus on development of trainer training programmes and career progression pathways for trainers have also not been defined.

Efforts in the skill landscape have been largely devoid of industry/employer linkages until the last few years. This has created gaps in terms of sectoral need and availability, competency required by employer and those possessed by a trainee etc. Placement of trainees has consequently suffered. While industry has started defining their skills requirements, and training methodology, commitments in terms of increased remuneration to skilled workers also need to be made by them. This is necessary to create economic incentive for skilling, and for industry to realize the productivity gains linked with skilled manpower.

Virtually every service sub-sector in the country is experiencing a severe shortage of skilled personnel on account of the booming conditions prevailing in service economy during the past few years. Shortages persist not only at the level of managers and supervisors but also at the level of skilled workmen in most sub-sectors. Thus, in healthcare there is a shortage of not only doctors and nurses but also of radiographers and laboratory technicians; in the hospitality sector there is dearth of hotel managers as well as of cooks and waiters; in IT and BPO services the need is not only for software specialists but also for simple graduates with some amount of fluency in the English language. In many cases the products of existing education and vocational training institutions are not fit for employment without undergoing further training while in others there is shortage of educational and training facilities. Expansion of technical and higher education and improvement in its quality will take care of some of the shortages but the vocational training requirements of the services sector need to be systematically addressed and given impetus through government initiative.

To sum up, there is need for skilling and re-skilling the persons entering the labour force to harness the demographic dividend that India enjoys. While the enrolment in technical higher education has grown, the employers continue to complain about non-availability of requisite number of skilled persons. This challenge needs to be addressed at the all-India as well as the State level in a mission mode manner, as otherwise the benefits of demographic dividend would be lost. The skill enhancement also leads to increased wages for the people and a positive growth outcome for the economy at large.

Skill development should, therefore, occupy centre-stage in any employment strategy. Skill development is critical for achieving faster, sustainable and inclusive growth on the one hand and for providing decent employment opportunities to the growing young population on the other. The demographic window of opportunity available to India would make India the skill capital of world. India would be in position to meet the requirement of technically trained manpower not only for its growing economy but also of the aging advanced economies of the world. Young population is an asset only if it is educated, skilled and finds productive employment. However, skilling this large and growing young population from an exceedingly small base would be a big challenge in terms of outreach, quality, and institutional set-ups.

The process of skill acquisition especially for the poor and needy persons should be made bankable. The effort should be to complement public investment with institutional/bank finance. The Central Ministries must focus on areas where private investment in skilled development is unlikely to be available or forthcoming. The Government should aim at useful public-private partnerships. The funds should be deployed more for activities than for buildings and other hard assets. However, upgradation of machinery and equipment, teaching and learning aids should be a continuous process. Creation of infrastructure in latest technology, need-based new initiatives, creation of infrastructure in rural, remote and difficult areas should continue. With fast changing skills in the labour market, focus should be on short, relevant and effective courses that would get candidates into the workplace.

Recent changes introduced by the Government have been with the purpose of providing greater coherence and coordination to skill development policies and programmes and to provide finance to worthy private sector initiatives.

**Endnotes**

1. Government of India, Planning Commission, *Twelfth Five Year Plan (2012-17)*, Volume III, Chapter 22, para 22.117.

2. Population growth and its relation to economic growth has been a matter of debate for a long time. The early Malthusian view was that population growth is likely to impede economic growth because it will put pressure on the available resources, result in reduction in per capita income and resources. This, in turn, will result in deterioration in quality of life. Contrary to the Malthusian predictions, several of the East Asian countries have been able to achieve economic prosperity and improvement in quality of life in spite of population growth. This has been attributed to the increase in productivity due to development and utilization of innovative technologies by the young educated population who formed the majority of the growing population. These countries have been able to exploit the dynamics of demographic transition to achieve economic growth by using the human resources as the engine driving the economic development. Improved employment with adequate emoluments has promoted saving and investment which, in turn, stimulated economic growth.
3. Government of India, Planning Commission, *An Approach to the Eleventh Five Year Plan*, November 2006, p. 5.
4. Government of India, Planning Commission, *An Approach to the Twelfth Five Year Plan*, October 2011, p. 5.

# Part II
## Science, Technology and Innovations

# 9

# Science and Technology in India

India has had a long and distinguished tradition in science and technology. In the half-century prior to Independence, India produced many scientists who achieved world renown. Generally, they were teacher-researchers in educational institutions.

### 9.1 Pre-Independence Period

Prior to Independence in 1947, little attention was given to the problem of scientific and industrial research in India. A number of universities and institutes carried out research, mostly on fundamental aspects of science. Certain industries also had their own research organisations. Industry depended, by and large, on foreign techniques and did not develop research programmes of its own. Hence, the industrial and technological base of the country was very small.

However, during the Second World War, India emerged as a major supply centre for the armed forces in the East. A large number of products which had been imported into the country had to be manufactured to meet both civilian and military needs. Indian substitutes had to be found for imported materials and processes had to be developed which would use these materials in place of imported ones. In these circumstances, the Government of India constituted the Board of Scientific and Industrial Research in 1940. The Council of Scientific and Industrial Research was formed in 1942. Much useful work was done under the auspices of these two bodies during the War. A number of problems, mostly related to military needs, were tackled and processes were developed for producing essential articles from indigenous materials.

After Independence, a scientific and technological infrastructure, covering a very broad spectrum of disciplines has been created. Scientific and technological accomplishments of significant magnitude have been seen in areas of high-technology like atomic energy, space and electronics. Closer to the lives of the masses, the success in attaining self-sufficiency in foodgrains production, based on genetic engineering, has been equally spectacular. Indian scientists and technologists have been able to fulfil national expectations when clear-cut objectives and tasks are indicated and necessary support provided. India has reaped ample rewards from the investments made in science and technology.

Over the years after Independence, a range of industries, from the small to the most sophisticated, has been established covering wide areas of utilities, services and goods, and a large number of technologists are now familiar with their operations. There is now a reservoir of expertise well acquainted with the most modern advances in basic and applied areas, and equipped to make choices between available technologies, readily absorb new technologies and provide a framework for future national development. Scientists and technologists have distinguished themselves not only in class rooms and laboratories but also in factories and fields, in conceptual planning and formulation of strategies and in their implementation. Indian scientists and technologists have demonstrated on many fronts that given clear-cut objectives and tasks and necessary support, they can fulfil national expectations.

The country has succeeded in creating a good base for scientific and industrial research. In agriculture, an integrated system involving research institutes, agricultural universities and an extension machinery has been set-up. In industry, there is a network of industrial research laboratories. Research and development divisions have been established in major enterprises and consultancy firms have come up for project consultancy and design engineering. The basis for this advance lies in the rapid expansion of higher and technical education. India now has the third largest scientific and technical workforce in the world. However, the country has still a long way to go to catch up with the better placed countries of the world. The ultimate aim of technological progress is improvement in productivity, efficiency in the use of basic resources like land, water and minerals and increase in income and employment.

The importance of developing science and technology in a major way has been recognised since Independence. The whole-hearted support provided to science and technology since then, has resulted in many accomplishments in a wide variety of disciplines. Moreover, these activities have played a dominant role in the socio-economic development of the country.

## 9.2 Importance of Science and Technology

The per capita income and quality of life that a nation enjoys is, in the final analysis, dependent largely on the technology it adopts, and which in turn has to be appropriate to its endowments, resources and skills.

The foundations of industrial and agricultural advance lie ultimately in the availability and effective use of human skills. Human skills are a formidable asset since they last not merely during one working life but because they are transmitted for generations. If these assets are used effectively, they may well turn out to be one of the most fruitful results of planning.

The pace of economic development depends on a variety of factors which constitute the psychological and sociological setting within which the economy operates. A major element in this setting is the community's will to progress and its readiness to develop and adopt new and more efficient methods and processes of production. Basically, development involves securing higher productivity all round and this is a function of the degree of technological advance the community is able to make. The problem is not one merely of adopting and applying the processes and techniques developed elsewhere, but of developing new techniques specially suited to local conditions.

Modern technology is changing rapidly and no country can hope to maintain a steady pace of advance unless it keeps abreast of current developments. Techniques in turn affect and are affected by economic and social organisation. Certain forms of economic and social organisation are unsuited to or incapable of absorbing new techniques and utilising them to the best advantage. To some extent techniques must of course be adapted to economic and social organisation, but the latter has also to change in order to accommodate new techniques which need to be applied not merely in one or two isolated lines but in several lines of economic activity.

The vital role of science in modern life is now generally recognised. Apart from the vast changes it has brought about, the development of a scientific temper in the people is considered important. Improvements in techniques evolved as a result of scientific research bring about great increases in production in the different sectors of the economy. National resources are augmented by the substitution of cheap and abundant materials for those in scarce supply and by finding uses for materials which have remained unutilised. A balanced programme of research covering every sector of the economy is essential therefore for the development of a country.

High standards of living in the more advanced countries are the direct result of progress in science and technology and the rapid pace of development associated with it. The flow of new scientific knowledge is continuous and ever expanding and covers both pure and applied research. Pure research leads to new knowledge and understanding of nature and its laws, and creates the scientific capital from which practical applications of knowledge are drawn. New products and processes are based on new principles and concepts. The advance of technology presents new problems to science and also provides new tools with which to resolve them.

India's development strategy has emphasised the need to develop skills at all levels. The basis for this is the rapid expansion of technical education. The number of students in engineering and technology colleges and industrial training institutes (ITIs) has increased sharply. The same picture holds true for other categories like scientists, doctors and agricultural graduates. In fact, India now has the third largest scientific and technical work force in the world. However, the capacity of the system to absorb fully these skills in productive employment has been less than adequate. In pure and applied research, advances have been limited except in a few areas like agricultural research, atomic energy and space.

### 9.3 Technology Upgradation

The level of technology and the concomitant levels of skills directly determine productivity of labour. Improvement of skill enhances labour productivity even with the existing technology. Labour productivity determines the potential relative shares of both labour and capital. Rise in labour productivity is a necessary condition for raising living standards of both wage and non-wage earners.

Potential for better wages of workers and remuneration of the self-employed and the living standards of the working poor increase *parri passu* with increased productivity of labour. Moreover, higher incomes and wages of the working poor would contribute to increased aggregate effective demand for goods and services produced, both in informal and formal sectors, stimulating investment and growth in both the sectors. Thus, a multiplier effect may result leading to faster growth all across.

Technology is one of the most critical elements in the growth of the small sector. India is ranked at the top in terms of availability of science and engineering personnel. However, small industries in India are loosing their competitive edge in the global markets due to lack of modern technology. Due to obsolete technology, cost of manufacturing is much higher than in the other developing countries in Asia. Addressing these problems to ensure a vibrant manufacturing sector is essential for sustained and inclusive growth.

The technique of production used in many small industries

like weaving and wood carving is obsolete. This has led to high production cost and output of inferior quality goods. Hence, modernisation of technology is urgently required to make small industries efficient.

Technology should be the foremost factor for enhancing the global competitiveness of Indian manufacturing sector. Without infusion of appropriate technology, survival in the global market place would be a question mark for a large majority of micro and small enterprises and even the medium enterprises.

The immediate challenge is development of appropriate technologies for various manufacturing processes which will lead to substantial reduction in cost of manufacturing by enhancing labour productivity, reducing material wastage and minimising energy consumption. Such technologies could be developed by close interaction of R&D institutions with industries and through innovative projects of technopreneurs. Accordingly, a multi-tier support system may be required for inducing technology-based competitiveness of the sector with the collaboration of government, industry clusters, industry associations and private R&D institutions. Liberal government policies and assistance are pre-requisites for nurturing innovative ideas both by academic institutions and technopreneurs.

The issue may be addressed by developing collaborations of public/private R&D institutions with the cluster/industry associations to take up R&D in focused areas of manufacturing with clear objectives, and project budget. This will ensure industry acceptability of the technology developed and delivery of the technology within the specified time frame. Government assistance may vary depending upon the level of the technology and the transaction cost involved and may be kept at an attractive level, especially for the projects taken up for technology development for nano-technology, aerospace, defence sector etc. to incentivize these sectors.

Competitive manufacturing technologies are available in

the international market for various industries. To facilitate absorption of such globally competitive technologies, government can subsidise the industry. Extent of support may again vary with the type of industry and the level of technology being adopted. MSMEs sector in India, with some exceptions, is characterised by low technology levels, which acts as a handicap in the emerging global market. As a result, sustainability of a large number of MSMEs will be in question in the face of competition from imported goods. Also MSMEs alliances with domestic large companies are fragile, since the large companies can themselves build alliances with overseas suppliers. Despite efforts, institutional linkages of R&D institutions and industry (including MSMEs) have not developed. Moreover, past policies on foreign direct investment (FDI) have not resulted in substantial technology gains percolating in the country.

Unregulated or haphazard application of modem techniques in all spheres of production is apt to create or aggravate technological unemployment. There is need for regulation here. This is not to suggest freezing of existing techniques. It only means that conditions have to be created in which modern techniques can be adopted in these lines of production and that the transition is orderly.

Technology development generally requires the setting up of clusters of industries that can share information and skills, as in *science parks* or dedicated industrial estates. Some such facilities exist in India, but their efficacy and functioning need to be strengthened.

## 9.4 Applications of Technological Advancement

Science and technology plays a crucial role in catalysing and accelerating economic and social development. It has an overarching impact in almost all sectors of the economy. It plays a lead role in contributing to sustainable development and self-reliance. It is now becoming increasingly clear that while the investments in physical infrastructure are important, it is the intellectual infrastructure derived through innovative initiatives that will give India a comparative advantage.

Science is an endless frontier, a unique human activity without limits. Massive support should be provided to basic research, especially in universities, so that India can contribute significantly towards advancing that frontier. While building on the comparative advantage that India possess in the emerging areas of information technology (IT) and biotechnology, special attention should be given to agriculture and agro-based industries and infrastructure sectors like energy, transportation, communication and housing.

**9.4.1 Small Industries:** The establishment of national laboratories and research institutes has a special importance in a country like India where medium and small-scale producers contribute a considerable proportion of industrial production. These industries cannot afford to have research facilities of their own, as the larger producers can. The research institutions will bring the fruits of research within their reach and enable them to reduce costs and improve the quality of their products. The establishment of these laboratories and institutes is thus complementary to the objective of promoting the development of micro, small and medium enterprises (MSMEs). In addition to these major research institutes, it is desirable to direct particular attention to the improvement of techniques in cottage industries. Such improvement may ultimately produce a far greater result all over the country than a limited number of large-scale industries.

**9.4.2 Technology and Rural Development:** Rural technology should not be taken to mean primitive technology or technology of yesterday. A determined effort is needed to take modern science and technology to the rural areas so that it is brought well within the material, financial and skill resources of rural people. Therefore, while searching for and improving upon such technologies which increase employment opportunities for the people, it will be simplistic and dangerous to confine indigenous efforts to relatively simple technology for rural needs and depend on import of technology in the high technology areas.

**9.4.3 Technology and Human Resources Development:** Technology can play a significant role in the promotion of human welfare. In the coming years, the benefits of technology must percolate more effectively to the vulnerable sections of the community and backward areas of the country.

In promoting the applications of science and technology for the benefit of the weaker sections, special programmes should be devised. A more coordinated and vigorous effort than in the past is needed to equip suitable persons from socially backward groups and weaker sections of the society to play a purposeful role in the area of technology.

High priority should be given to technologies that are oriented towards human welfare. These include technologies that provide creative and cost-effective solutions in health services, population management, mitigating the effects of natural hazards, conservation of land, water and energy resources and their integrated management for sustainable development.

Human resource development in science and technology is an area of concern today. The declining popularity of science and the unwillingness among the youth to take up science as a career will jeopardise India's future. Imaginative and innovative programmes need to be undertaken to attract the students to science and technology and enhance the number of young scientists.

**9.4.4 Space Science:** The thrust of the Indian space programme has been to develop skills and capabilities to design and build satellites and satellite launch vehicles; to define areas of application such as telecommunication, broadcasting and remote sensing, and to design and fabricate instrumentation for such applications; and to commission and utilise operational application systems to ensure the benefits of space science and technology for the socio-economic development of the nation. The Indian space programmes are directed towards the goal of achieving self-reliance in the use of space technology for national development.

There is export potential for providing ground systems, products, satellite and launch vehicle systems, satellite services and launch services on a commercial basis to other countries, which will make the Indian space engineering industry a more viable proposition in the years to come. Indian exports today derive their competitive advantage on the basis of cheap labour and abundance of natural resources. The Indian export basket does not have a significant amount of technologically-intensive products. This situation needs to change. Therefore, emphasis should be on the export of high-tech products and export of technology.

**9.4.5 Biotechnology:** The primary objective in this discipline should be to develop products and processes/technologies, whose large-scale applications would result in societal benefits in the sectors of health, agriculture, animal resources development, aquaculture, energy, environment and forests and industry. The strategy should involve the development of specialized manpower and infrastructure for these programmes and a very strong base of R&D.

There has been a significant growth in India's capability as also its accomplishments in several high technology areas such as nuclear and space science and technology, electronics and defence research and development. Many new programmes and initiatives are envisaged in these, so as to ensure: (a) growth in these strategic and vital sectors, (b) operationalisation of projects or programmes that have been successfully demonstrated and (c) transfer of technology to other sectors, particularly in the broader production sector.

There have also been significant developments and achievements in science and technology related to the sectors with large societal implications such as in agriculture. Efforts have been mounted for developing newly emerging key areas e.g. microelectronics, informatics/telematics, biotechnology, new materials, renewable energy sources, ocean sciences and several areas of basic research. A large base has been created in the areas of biological and industrial research which needs to be consolidated, expanded and utilized.

### 9.5 Utilisation of Scientific Research

India's development plans have consistently emphasised the need for sustained investment in research and related activities leading to creation of substantial capacity and capabilities in science and technology. The fruits of this effort are evident in India's nuclear and space programmes, information and communication technology services, automotive and pharmaceuticals industries and other areas. As the Indian economy continues on the path of rapid, more inclusive and sustainable growth, it will be necessary to ensure that India's capabilities in science and technology grow in strength. This is especially important if India is to become one of the major economies of the world in the near future.

The importance of ensuring speedy and extensive utilisation on a commercial scale of the results of scientific research has been stressed for several years. However, a large proportion of the inventions made in the country still remain to be exploited. Intervals between the time when the results of laboratory research become available and their wider application, are at present considerable and there is need for more effective action. The rapid utilisation of the results of research is hindered on account of inadequate liaison between industry and research organisations.

The same lags in the utilisation of the results of research which appear in industry are also found in other fields of development such as transport, construction and power. Promising results are secured and new designs, techniques and specifications are evolved. For lack of extended application, due possibly to conservatism or inertia, full value is not realised from expenditures incurred on research, thereby slowing down the process of technical advance and modernisation.

**9.5.1 Academia-Industry Linkages:** It is desirable to

develop industry-oriented institutions as centres of excellence in selected areas. Such centres should be set up in selected fields around industry, in close association with the academic institutions and national laboratories. It has long been recognised that creative work cannot be administered or controlled in the same manner as general administration.

Linkages between academic institutions on the one hand and national scientific agencies, laboratories and public sector enterprises on the other, have to be strengthened. This can be done in several ways such as through increased mobility of scientific personnel between education and research organisations, joint research projects, and insistence on a minimum percentage of the R&D budget of government scientific agencies and public sector enterprises being spent in the academic sector. Universities and colleges should also be encouraged to undertake applied research, useful for several regions of the country. Since the problems of a particular region are unique and intrinsic the best way to find solutions to those regional problems would be to make use of the local resources—people, scientists and community at large.

## 9.6 Challenges for the Future

India has unique challenges and large unmet needs across diverse areas such as health, education, skills, agriculture, urban and rural development, energy and so on. It also has significant challenges of exclusion and inequitable access due to multiple deprivations of class, caste and gender—all of which require innovative approaches and solutions, and looking beyond the conventional way of doing things. Innovation is going to be central to providing answers to the most pressing challenges and for creating opportunity structures for sharing the benefits of the emerging knowledge economy. Affordable solutions, innovative business models or processes which ease delivery of services to citizens can enable more people to join the development process.

**9.6.1 Upgrading Institutions of Higher Learning:** The

higher education institutions with their research facilities are a unique base for the training of competent scientists and technologists. However, with the rapid expansion of the number of institutions and students, without the corresponding inputs by way of facilities, the role of universities as advanced centres of teaching and research has been eroded, leading not only to the weakening of science teaching and research but also adversely affecting the climate so essential for higher learning. The need today is, therefore, to restore to the universities their proper image as centres of higher learning. Although it would be unrealistic to expect all the members of the academic community to take up research in addition to teaching, there is an urgent need to integrate teaching and research so that universities present a different image and are restored to their recognised position.

Facilities available in universities are not adequate. That they should be increased cannot be overemphasised. It is in the general interest of not only the universities, but also scientific agencies, public enterprises and technical departments in the Centre and the States, that the resources in the education sector are considerably augmented, since the manpower that they need comes from the university sector.

There is widespread concern regarding the quality and extent of the technology base in the country. Engineering education and research need significant support. It would be necessary to establish a mechanism which will enable funds from research stations regionally distributed, or created for sectors of industry in cooperation with industry. The mechanical and electronic engineering areas require immediate attention. There is need to establish a mechanism which will enable funds from Government as well as from industry, including the public and private sectors, to be received and used for engineering research.

Unless a true enthusiasm for science is generated during school and college stages, even the very intelligent and scientifically minded, who would achieve much in science, would turn to safer and more lucrative professions, as is already happening. Government has to be particularly sensitive in spotting talent and creativity, wherever it exists and providing opportunities for its emergence.

**9.6.2 Selecting Thrust Areas:** There are major new areas in science and technology emerging on the world scene as, for example micro-electronics, informatics and telematics, robotics, biotechnologies, material sciences, oceanography, instrumentation, several areas in chemistry, modern biology and earth sciences and space technologies. These should be reorganised as thrust areas and should receive significant support.

India is a large country faced with a broad and complex range of problems. With the present constraints of fiscal and human resources, it would not be possible to deal with all the problems or all areas of science and technology at the same time. Therefore, there has to be a degree of selectivity and allocation of priorities. There is need to not only define areas of strength for consolidation and development, but also areas of weakness that require corrective action, together with identification of gaps, particularly in newly emerging areas of great promise.

**9.6.3 Percolation of Technology to Grassroots:** There has been a tendency to regard science and technology as a separate and compartmentalised activity, to be carried out in universities, in research laboratories and in large specialised scientific institutions. It is not generally realised that science and technology should be an integral and essential part of all sectors of the national activity. The results of science and technology are yet to be felt in terms of a major impact on the economic development, improvement in the quality of life of the people and in the availability of better goods and services. During the coming years it should be ensured that the efforts in science and technology are not confined in laboratories and academic institutions but percolate to the grassroots levels so that science, technology and innovations increasingly become part of the life of the people. For this, appropriate mechanisms and management practices would need to be introduced.

**9.6.4 Indigenous Development of Technology:** Issues of natural resource conservation and agricultural growth cannot be effectively tackled in the absence of an appropriate technological base. In addition, technology is essential for increasing the competitiveness of the Indian economy in international markets. Indigenous development of technology is therefore of the highest importance and deliberate planned steps need to be taken to increase technological self-sufficiency of the country.

Rapid technical progress is altering fundamentally the skills, knowledge, infrastructure and institutions needed for the efficient production and delivery of goods and services. So broad and far-reaching are current technological developments that many see the emergence of another industrial revolution driven by a new technological paradigm. This paradigm involves not only new technologies and skills in the traditional sense, but also different work methods, management techniques and organisational relations within firms. As new transport and communications technologies shrink international economic space, it also implies a significant reordering of comparative advantage, and trade and investment relations, between countries.

Experience of many developing and industrialised countries suggests that a rapid acceleration of industrial technology development calls for a deliberate strategy, in the sense that it requires the government to coordinate and guide an essentially market-driven process.

**9.6.5 Coherent Technology Strategy:** Indian technology policies are undergoing significant changes, and on the whole have improved greatly in recent years. They are not, however, ideal. A coherent technology strategy in India must address a number of interconnected elements in the incentive regime and the relevant factor markets and institutions.

Technology development calls for both general and specific forms of human capital, and emerging technologies are highly skill-intensive in both technical and managerial terms. While India is endowed at present with large amounts of high-level human capital, investments in the creation of new skills—as measured by enrolment levels in technical subjects at all levels—are low. In addition, firm level investments in training are highly variable, and large parts of industry invest very little in training. The small industrial sector in particular suffers from very low levels of skill, while industrial training institutes are often unresponsive to their needs.

**9.6.6 Technology Information and Dissemination Services:** Technology upgrading requires that Indian enterprises of all types have information on relevant technologies in international markets and also within the country. Many countries have well-developed systems of computerised on-line technology information and dissemination services, often backed up with consultancy and financial assistance for small and medium enterprises to enable them to know about, test, and implement new technologies. The availability of similar facilities is weak in India. Note needs to be taken of the emerging trends of restrictions on access to technology through stringent intellectual property restrictions and on dual use technologies by certain groups of industrially advanced countries. Special efforts have to be made both at national as well as at international levels, to ensure that such restrictions do not inhibit progress in high technology sectors.

Technology development generally requires the setting up of clusters of industries that can share information and skills, as in *science parks* or dedicated industrial estates. Some such facilities exist in India, but their efficacy and functioning need to be strengthened.

**9.6.7 Funding Pattern:** Government has so far been the main source of funding science and technology activities in the country. This needs to be significantly supplemented by the industry.

The challenge is how to create a vibrant landscape of public private partnership and an enabling framework for attracting investment from the industrial sector into R&D system and incentivize the same for linking development with deployment in the innovation and technology sector.

While India is amongst the top recipients in Asia for venture funds and private equity funds so far, these investments need to be focused on small early stage start-ups and not only into relatively large and safer investments.

The corporate sector, in particular, must play a much larger role in building research capability as happens in other countries.

The pace of scientific and technological research in more advanced countries has .greatly increased. In the economy of these countries, scientific research has an important and honoured place and receives every encouragement. As the field of enquiry and investigation widens, larger funds are invested and there is intense search for scientific talent. One of the results of this activity in the more advanced countries, however, has been that the gap between the advanced and less advanced countries tends to become ever larger. The task before India is to cover this distance by putting in the utmost effort in the development of scientific and technological research, and in the application of science in the furtherance of her development programmes. Investment in scientific research will make a large and enduring contribution to the prosperity of the country.

**9.6.8 Involvement of States:** The involvement of States in R&D in the country is at present relatively low. Most States have not established suitable mechanisms for full utilisation of technologies emanating from public-funded research in the country. State Councils for science and technology in many States remain as weak links between the national science sector and the State Governments. Allocation of States in their own budgets for science and technology remains relatively insignificant. Special mechanisms need to be developed to promote the technology relationships between the Centre and the States. Establishment of special competitive fund for States for absorption of indigenous technologies could form one of the strategies for creating demand pull for technologies in the States.

To face up to the increasing challenges in the new world order, the Indian science and technology landscape needs to undergo a paradigm shift. It needs to evolve new delivery mechanisms for innovative deployment of technologies and business models for financing deployment of innovations. This calls for a well-enunciated science, technology and innovation policy.

A competitive knowledge economy must be built on the pillars of: (a) an educational system that produces human resources which are employable and globally benchmarked, (b) science and technology pursued on an enormous scale to generate knowledge for long-term use and (c) strategic translational research inspired by national needs and global opportunities.

It is necessary to establish linkages between the different sectors of education, scientific research, technology development, productive activities in agriculture, industry etc. and government decision-making structures.

To sum up, science and technology is widely recognised as an important tool for fostering and strengthening the economic and social development of the country. India has made significant progress in various spheres of science and technology over the years and can now take pride in having a strong network of technical institutions, trained manpower and an innovative knowledge base. Given the rapid pace of globalisation, fast-depleting material resources, increasing competition among nations and the growing need to protect intellectual property, the importance of strengthening the knowledge base is an important issue that needs to be recognised.

It must be borne in mind that scientific explorations and widening the frontiers of knowledge are important activities of all civilised societies. India has had its own treasure house of traditional sciences. India has produced many giants in a variety of disciplines of science during the 20th century. It must be ensured that creativity and excellence are nurtured amongst the younger generation and India contributes to future discoveries and inventions on a scale that is appropriate for its size and history.

India has made a substantial progress in a number of areas related to the economy, viz. food security, average life expectancy, literacy and higher education. However, one cannot be complacent about these achievements, as growth towards excellence is a continuous process and there is need to mount efforts to control population and improve the levels of food security, economic growth, literacy, health and so on, apart from realising the technological strengths in the emerging global industrial and economic environment by optimal utilisation of science and technology system in the country, which provides immense opportunities and offers great challenges.

In addition to R&D in high science and strategic technology areas that would enable the country to position itself at the world level, there are several areas that require significant science and technology inputs to generate solutions for issues that are significant for the country's development goals, in the context of both industrial development and rural development. These include energy, water and sanitation, farm production, health care, waste disposal, computing and communications, e-infrastructure, cyber security and so on.

The Indian R&D system is predominantly government funded. It is important that the corporate sector (both public and the private) come forward to fund R&D programmes directed towards national developmental goals.

# 10

# Science, Technology and Innovation (STI) Policy, 2013

Science, technology and innovation (STI) have emerged as the major drivers of national development globally. As India aspires for faster, sustainable and inclusive growth, the Indian STI system, with the advantages of a large demographic dividend and the huge talent pool, will need to play a defining role in achieving these national goals. The national STI enterprise must become central to national development.

India's Scientific Policy Resolution (SPR) of 1958 resolved to "foster, promote and sustain" the "cultivation of science and scientific research in all its aspects". Technology was then expected to flow from the country's established science infrastructure. The Technology Policy Statement (TPS) of 1983 emphasized the need to attain technological competence and self-reliance. The Science and Technology Policy (STP) of 2003 brought science and technology (S&T) together and emphasized the need for investment in R&D. It called for integrating programmes of socio-economic sectors with the national R&D system to address national problems as well as creating a national innovation system.

Presently, innovation is no longer a mere appendage to science and technology but has assumed centre stage in the developmental goals of countries around the world. Vertical integration of all dimensions of STI into the socio-economic processes seems the way forward in the modern world. New paradigms of innovation have emerged and systems that foster innovation are not universal. They have become country and context specific.

## 10.1 Objectives of STI Policy, 2013

The Prime Minister unveiled the Science, Technology and Innovation (STI) Policy, 2013 at the inaugural session of the Centenary session of the Indian Science Congress in Kolkatta on January 3, 2013.

STI Policy seeks to send a signal to the Indian scientific community, both in the private and public domain, that *science, technology and innovation should focus on faster, sustainable and inclusive development of the people*. The policy seeks to focus on both *STI for people and people for STI.* It aims to bring all the benefits of science, technology and innovation to the national development and sustainable and more inclusive growth. It seeks the right sizing of the gross expenditure on research and development by encouraging and incentivizing private sector participation in R&D, technology and innovation activities.

The policy also seeks to trigger an ecosystem for innovative abilities to flourish by leveraging partnerships among diverse stakeholders and by encouraging and facilitating enterprises to invest in innovations. It also seeks to bring in mechanisms for achieving gender parity in STI activities and gaining global competitiveness in select technological areas through international cooperation and alliances. The policy goal is to accelerate the pace of discovery, diffusion and delivery of science led solutions for serving the aspirational goals of India for faster, sustainable and inclusive growth.

A strong and viable Science, Research and Innovation System for High Technology-led path for India (SRISHTI) is a goal of STI policy.

## 10.2 Main Features of STI Policy, 2013

**10.2.1 Policy for Science and Science Policy for Development: A New Paradigm:** Science, research and innovation can exist separately on their own in disconnected spaces. But there are synergistic linkages. India's global competitiveness will be determined by the extent to which the STI enterprise integrates vertically and is able to create social good and economic good through innovation. Innovative structural mechanisms and models will thus need to be evolved to balance the priorities and develop interconnections of the three sectors.

India's STI system needs to deliver solutions to address the pressing national challenges of energy and food security, nutrition, affordable health care, environment, water and sanitation and above all employment. Thus, discovery and solution dimensions of science and technology need to play major roles in shaping the future of the country. "Science and technology for the people" will be the new paradigm of the Indian STI enterprise. Indian society must emerge as the major stake holder for the national STI system.

India's STI-led developmental efforts should thus aim at faster, inclusive and sustainable growth. While global competitiveness in trade would call for high technology inputs, inclusive growth would need to ensure access, availability and affordability of solutions to as large a population as possible. India needs 'inclusive innovation'. The policy will thus drive both investment in science and investment of science-led technology and innovation in agriculture, manufacturing and services that lead to socio-economic benefits to a wide cross section of society. Emphasis will be laid on bridging the gaps between knowledge and the economic sectors. The STI policy would develop symbiotic relationship with economic and other policies.

**10.2.2 Capturing Aspirations:** The key elements of the STI policy will be:

1. Promoting proliferation of scientific temper amongst all sections of society.
2. Enhancing skill for applications of science among the young from all social strata
3. Making careers in science, research and innovation attractive to the brightest.

4. Establishing world class R&D infrastructure for gaining global leadership in some select frontier areas of science.
5. Positioning India among the top five global scientific powers by 2020.
6. Linking contributions of science, research and innovation system with inclusive economic growth agenda and combine priorities of excellence with relevance.
7. Migrating R&D outputs into commercial applications by replicating hitherto successful models as well as establishment of new structures.
8. Facilitating S&T-based high-risk innovations through new mechanisms.
9. Triggering changes in the mindset and value systems to recognize, respect and reward performances which create wealth from S&T derived knowledge.

**10.2.3 Investment in Research and Development:** Global investments in science, technology and innovation are estimated at US$ 1.2 trillion as of 2009. India's R&D investment is less than 2.5 percent of the global investments. India's R&D investment has been under 1 percent of the GDP. Increasing Gross Expenditure in Research and Development (GERD) to 2 percent of the GDP has been a national goal for some time. Achieving this in the next five years is realizable provided the private sector matches India's public investment and the ratio of public to private sector investments in R&D changes from the current 3:1 to 1:1 within the next five years. This seems attainable as the industrial R&D investment grew by 250 percent while the sales growth was at 200 percent between 2005 and 2010. An environment conducive for enhancing private sector investment in R&D will be created.

Gross budgetary support for the science and technology sector has significantly increased during the last decade. Accrual of benefits of such increase in the GERD is becoming evident. India's global share of scientific publications has, for example, increased from 1.8 percent in 2001 to 3.5 percent in 2011. The composite annual growth rate (CAGR) of Indian publications during the last three years is around 12±1 percent. But the percentage of Indian publications in the top 1 percent impact making journals is only 2.5 percent.

India should aim to increase its share of scientific publications from the current 3.5 percent to over 7 percent and quadruple the number of papers in top 1 percent journals from the current levels by 2020. Citation impact of Indian publications must improve and match at least the global averages. Initiatives under the new policy should enable this to exceed the global average by 2020.

India ranks ninth globally in the number of scientific publications and 12th in the number of patents filed. According to the Global Science Report of the UNESCO, India's current global ranking matches with its ranking with respect to the number of Full-Time Equivalent (FTE) of R&D personnel. In order to match the enhanced level of private sector investments in R&D and to maintain the tempo of public sector investments, it is imperative that within the next five years the total number of FTE of R&D personnel must increase by at least 66 percent of the present strength.

**10.2.4 Nourishing the Root of Science for Promoting Excellence in Research:** Ensuring sustainable pipeline of talented youth for science is a challenge. India has mounted some significant initiatives for attracting talent to science and careers with research. Empowering stakeholders for local actions is a key element of these initiatives. The policy framework will further enable school science education through improvement of teaching methods and science curricula, motivating science teachers and schemes for early attraction of talent to science.

**10.2.5 Combining Excellence and Relevance: Way Forward for Indian Science:** Basic research-led discoveries stimulate innovation in the long term. While Indian investment in basic research will be further enhanced by fostering excellence through global benchmarks and focusing on relevance for addressing national challenges.

The few inter-university centres set up earlier have proved the concept to be a successful and viable one. Such inter-university centres would be multiplied in different fields to enable a wide cross section of university researchers to access advanced research facilities and equipment which are otherwise not available in university environments. Grand challenge programmes, where resource deployment could bring tangible and intangible returns in the global setting, will be launched.

**10.2.6 Participation in Creation of Large Global R&D Infrastructures and Big Science:** Modern science is increasingly becoming resource intensive. There is a current trend to create high-cost global infrastructures through international consortia models. Given India's global standing in science, invitation to participate in such projects is expected to increase. Indian participation in such consortia-led international projects will be encouraged and facilitated for improving access to facilities for advanced research in cutting edge areas of science.

**10.2.7 Attracting Private Sector Investments in R&D**: Supply side interventions have hitherto been the main strategy for public investment in R&D. The situation requires changing; equal emphasis on both supply side interventions and demand based investments is needed. While public investments in R&D should maintain the current rates of growth, private investment has to increase significantly for translating R&D outputs into commercial outcomes.

Public funds for partnerships with the private sector for social and public good objectives will be earmarked as a new policy initiative. A National Science, Technology and Innovation Foundation will be established as a public-private-partnership (PPP) initiative for investing critical levels of resources for innovative and ambitious projects.

The focus of the policy environment will be:

1. Facilitating private sector investment in R&D centres in India and overseas.

2. Permitting multi stakeholders participation in the Indian R&D system.
3. Treating R&D in the private sector at par with public institutions for availing public funds.
4. Bench marking of R&D funding mechanisms and patterns globally.
5. Aligning Venture Capital and Inclusion Innovation Fund systems.
6. Modifying IPR policy to provide for marching rights for social good when supported by public funds and for co-sharing IPRs generated under PPP.
7. Exploring newer mechanisms for fostering technology business incubators (TBIs) and science-led entrepreneurship.
8. Providing incentives for commercialization of innovations with focus on green manufacturing.

**10.2.8 Partnerships among Stakeholders for Scaling Successes of R&D**: Special and innovative mechanisms for leveraging academia-research-industry partnerships will be devised. Success stories in S&T-based innovations from Indian experience would be replicated and scaled up. Regulatory and legal framework for sharing of IPRs between inventors and investors, and for closing gaps in the translation of new findings into the commercial space, would be put in place. Specifically the policy will focus on:

1. Prioritizing critical R&D areas like agriculture, telecommunications, energy, water management, drug discovery, material science including nano technology, climate change and space technology and promoting interdisciplinary research.
2. Promoting innovations through mechanisms including "Small Idea-Small Money" and "Risky Idea Fund" to support innovation incubators.
3. Supporting STI driven entrepreneurship with high scaling coefficients and viable business models.
4. Investing in young innovators and entrepreneurs through education and training.

**10.2.9 Gaining Global Competitiveness through Collaboration**: Open source discoveries for public and social good form interesting innovation systems. Knowledge commons is an emerging theme for managing IPRs created through multi-stake holder participation. The STI Policy will foster data sharing and access. Tapping global resources and especially Indian Diaspora for accelerating the pace of technology-led development would be pursued. Multi-sectoral partnerships and alliances will be leveraged for up-scaling national competitiveness in research and manufacturing. The new policy framework will enable strategic partnerships and alliances with other nations through both bilateral and multilateral cooperation in science, technology and innovation. Cooperation in areas like climate change and mitigating natural disasters are important and beneficial. Science diplomacy, technology synergy and technology acquisition models should be judiciously deployed based on strategic relationships.

**10.2.10 Performance-Reward Relationships**: Transparent systems for tracking individual research performers based on past and proven track record would be developed to enable grant based investments in such performers. A well-designed centrally implementable Performance Related Incentive Scheme (PRIS) for basic research leading to scientific publications would be put in place.

For R&D leading to technology development and knowledge services, the criteria would, however, be specific to the institution, the local conditions and the context. Incentives to public-funded R&D centres for outcomes leading to public and strategic goods could be introduced. Transparent performance-reward relationships and accountability for investments would form central theme of the policy.

**10.2.11 Leveraging Innovation Potentials for Social Inclusion**: Global innovations systems tend to bypass large sections of the community. The instruments of the STI policy will aim at increasing accessibility, availability and affordability of innovations. Establishment of a Fund for Innovations for Social Inclusion will be a step in this direction.

**10.2.12 Delivery Systems for STI Outputs to Stakeholders and Society:** Migration of scientific outputs and technology interventions into the social systems is a multi-layered process. Direct delivery of scientific outputs through dissemination and public outreach by the scientific agencies and bodies is possible only in relatively smaller number of sectors. The entire delivery mechanism involves a large number of intermediaries from the public, nongovernmental and private sectors. This requires strengthening of linkages between the scientific and socio-economic sectors. The STI policy will leverage the R&D allocations of socio-economic ministries through a shared vision on addressing developmental challenges, co-generation of values through partnerships, and co-investments, adoption of new delivery models and maximization of stakeholder value perceptions.

The State Governments constitute important stake holders and measures will be taken to ensure that state-specific S&T vision and plans are informed by the new STI Policy.

**10.2.13 Transition from Perception to Evidence-based Approaches for Investment Decisions:** Sound measurement principles for STI indicators are necessary for evidence based policy actions. New and globally relevant indicators, which integrate measures of excellence with relevance as well as inventiveness with affordability, will be developed. Around 10 sectors of high impact potential, with commitment to deploy commensurate resources, will be identified for directed STI intervention. Enabling policy instruments that facilitate both research and enterprise to focus their efforts in these will be put in place.

Global competitiveness of manufacturing sector is closely related to the technology intensity of the sector, which in turn is a direct corollary of the vitality of the R&D system in providing technology inputs. India's share of global trade in high technology products is presently only around 8 percent.

The aim is to double this share through innovations in high-technology products. Appropriate supporting instruments will be put in place to stimulate the development and deployment of high technology by industry.

**10.2.14 Triggering Ecosystem Changes for Science, Technology and Innovation:** A flexible approach that allows for fine tuning the Five Year Plan investments in R&D, technology and innovation in response to rapid changes in STI ecosystem would be put in place. Speed, scale and sustainability would be key governance parameters for the new approach. Internal processes of institutions need to build-in Trust as an integral principle in decision making. "Risks" are integral parts of a vibrant national innovation system and policies must provide for risk management strategies. Education is currently focused on understanding; it should now embrace emphasis on Applications as well. Venture capital systems need to adventure in risky innovations rather than to rely on incremental innovations, new financing mechanisms for investing in enterprises without fear of failure and options for foreclosing unsuccessful ventures are essential part of such an enabling innovation ecosystem. India's innovation machinery should aim to lead rather than to follow safe paths of discovery. Hence trust, risk, application, venture, enterprise and leadership should form new mantras of the new STI ecosystem.

**10.2.15 Gender Parity in STI Sector:** Participation of women in STI activities is important. New and flexible schemes would be put in place to address the mobility challenges of employed women scientists and technologists. A broad scope for re-entry of women into R&D and new facilitation mechanisms with special career path in diverse areas will also be made feasible.

**10.2.16 Public Awareness and Public Accountability of Indian STI Sector:** Public understanding of science is an important dimension for introducing and reaching the benefits of modern science and technology to the people. Public and political understanding of science should be based on evidence and debates with open mind. The civilizational aspect of science or scientific temper needs to be promoted across all sections of the society systematically. People and decision makers must be made aware of the implications of emerging technologies, including their ethical, social and economic dimensions. Effective science communication methods, by using tools such as the National Knowledge Network, will be initiated. These will enable all the stakeholders of the civil society to discuss and present a collective perspective on such developments. Mechanisms for assessing the performance of the national STI system by all the stakeholders and reporting to the nation on a periodic basis will be established. The national science academies will be accorded a major role in this endeavour of public accountability.

**10.2.17 Science, Technology and Innovation to Serve National Agenda:**

1. **Agriculture:** R&D policy for agriculture is articulated by the Indian Council of Agriculture Research (ICAR). Integration of the agriculture R&D policy with the national R&D system and STI policy will be brought about.
2. **Manufacturing:** STI inputs to manufacturing sector offer opportunities for enhanced employment generation. A strategic selection of sectors, where India can aspire for leadership, would be made for focused STI inputs. A special drive for stepping up R&D intensity in key manufacturing sectors with competitive advantage will be mounted. Small and Medium Enterprises (SME) generally have low R&D intensity. Special schemes to support R&D at the firm or collective level, will be devised and put in place.
3. **Services:** The R&D intensity of the service sector needs to be enhanced considerably and skill base also expanded significantly. Linkages between the services with educational sectors for establishing human capacities will be fostered through incentive mechanisms. For rapidly

accomplishing the tasks of modernization of technology-led services, technology missions, aimed at achieving global leadership in some select areas in the services sector, will be identified. Deployment of technology-led services for increasing transparency in the Government machinery will also be supported.

4. **Climate Change:** Climate change is of global concern and India has articulated a National Action Plan for Climate Change (NAPCC). The S&T system will have to play an active role as a source of strategic knowledge for coping with the challenges of climate change as well as in meeting equity-based differentiated and shared responsibilities of India.

**10.2.18 Policy Goal:** STI Policy, 2013, is focused on serving India by connecting performance with excellence and relevance. The policy goal of the Indian STI sector is to accelerate the pace of discovery and delivery of science-led solutions for serving the aspirational goals of India for faster, sustainable and inclusive growth. Aspirations of India would be serviced by an equally aspiring Indian STI system.

# 11

# Innovations: Conceptual Settings

## 11.1 Innovation Defined

Scientific research utilizes money to generate knowledge and, by providing solutions, innovation converts knowledge into wealth and/or value. Innovation thus implies S&T-based solutions that are successfully deployed in the economy or the society. It has assumed centre stage in the developmental goals of nations. Paradigms of innovation have become country and context specific.

Science has played a key role in enhancing the growth and development of society and generating access to new and improved goods and services. Science underpins most breakthrough initiatives, but beyond the domain of science, innovations play a critical role in enhancing delivery of services and enabling access to improved goods. In view of this, emerging economies need to stimulate and strengthen its entire formal scientific and industrial system as well as the innovation system to develop solutions for the country's agenda of faster, sustainable and more inclusive growth.

Innovation is a process whereby people or groups of people with an entrepreneurial mindset (organizations, enterprises) develop new ideas or absorb and adapt existing ones. Together with institutions and policies that affect their behaviour and performance, they create new products, processes, and forms of organization. Innovation is not only about scientists in laboratories, theoretical science, or new discoveries. It is about building the capacity to find solutions to practical everyday development problems. So, an innovative economy is marked by ideas for new products or new ways of doing things and transforming them into profitable products or activities.

Joseph Schumpeter, an American economist, was one of the first academicians to study the idea of innovation. He developed a theory of economic and social change which focused on the importance of innovation and the factors influencing it. He suggested an important distinction between invention and innovation. According to him, invention is the first occurrence of the idea for a new product or process while innovation occurs when the idea is put into practice.

## 11.2 Importance of Innovations

Bringing about innovation has never been as important as today, as the global economy shifts away from the industrial economy towards the innovation economy. Traditional manufacturing is becoming increasingly commoditized while intellectual property is the need of the hour. What is heartening is that recent economic theory suggests that government investment in R&D, knowledge-creation, and technological progress does have a role to play in fuelling innovation, productivity, capital creation, and therefore growth. This thinking highlights the scope for appropriate government policy and investment to enable entrepreneurship and innovation.

Innovation can play a very important role in the development discourse, because it can offer a new approach to a system that is currently over-burdened by the multiple demands and has limited resources at its disposal. Enhanced focus on innovation can have an impact in diverse areas such as health and education delivery, governance, enterprise development and much more. Collectively, this can herald a generational change in the country and can lay out a chart for a more sustainable and inclusive growth paradigm.

For countries to make the next big move—from developing the right skills demanded by the market to dynamically improving the quality and quantity of that demand—developing an innovation system is critical.

### 11.3 Skills Required for Innovations

Innovations can come in various forms. They encompass the products, processes, and services that meet market needs. They may be developed and marketed in the manufacturing sector, but they may also apply to new ways of doing things in all sectors, including commerce and service delivery. And the innovative idea needs to be widely tested and applied by those who have the skills and financing to bring it to scale. This calls for engaging those with marketing and managerial skills and venture capital.

Research is important—but not always central—to innovation, which may also be realized through less technical experimentation and discovery. The use of cell phones to provide banking services across India is an example both of developing cheap handsets and communication networks and adapting the technology to non-traditional use.

Innovation—and thus growth—can be encouraged by three human development–related factors, and the accompanying policies that facilitate them. First, individuals need a range of skills. Second, these skills and the ideas flowing from them have to be connected to others. Third, productivity increases when innovative small business owners can grow with the aid of risk management tools or as innovative skilled workers enter the labour market. This three-part process is relevant to all individuals despite their starting points.

Three types of skills are necessary to unlock creative potential and take it to market.

1. The general skills are necessary to adapt existing technologies, compete in an innovation-driven economy, and manage the increasingly networked innovation process. These skills include basic literacy and numeracy, problem-solving, and social and interpersonal skills.
2. Creativity produces new ideas. Innovative thinkers are curious and persevering and have *divergent thinking*—imagining several responses to a single problem rather than converging to a single, right answer.

3. Entrepreneurial skills range from managerial skills in running a business to motivation. These are the skills to sort out good ideas from bad ones, find the resources and means to create a prototype, and take the idea through its growth phases. Education and training systems can teach individuals to be cognitively developed, creative, and entrepreneurial.

Both creativity and entrepreneurial skills can be incorporated into teaching methodologies at all points of the skill formation process. And education systems can encourage innovation-related specialties, such as math, science, and business and managerial skills. But these strategies will be successful only if education systems improve the quality of the basic mathematics and science skills for the majority of students. Without such a basis, efforts to instil risk-taking and entrepreneurial skills will be wasted.

Innovation cannot realize its full potential if innovators are isolated. The innovator needs other creative and skilled individuals to share ideas with and bring those ideas to market, capital to finance the realization of the idea, and an enabling environment that accepts new ideas.

In the knowledge economy, universities as a source of knowledge have become far more important than in the past. In recent years, they have acquired a crucial *third mission*, of contributing to economic development after teaching and research. Among the developed countries, the United States is feted for offering entrepreneurs many structural advantages, among them close linkages with universities. Many universities have incubators, technology parks, and venture funds within their sprawling campuses. Similarly, in Cambridge, UK, engagement of the faculty with industry has spawned many *millionaire dons*. The private sector can be tapped to fund research and development at universities.

Effective mechanisms of collaboration need to be created for universities and industry bodies so that research output and innovations can effectively be commercialized and transformed into marketable products and services for last mile benefits. A cluster-based approach to spur innovations at universities could be adopted wherein a minimum critical mass of universities is identified and efforts are made to create or strengthen the innovation system around them. The innovation universities could also provide a platform for experimenting with new models of universities where the above mentioned integration could be realized.

Collaborations can play a crucial role in stimulating innovations and fostering knowledge transfers which would foster interconnections that link intellectual, financial, human, and creative capital as well as unleash underutilized capital. Such enterprises could take the shape of physical or virtual clusters, which bring together research, business, risk capital, and creativity to turn ideas into products, processes, and services.

## 11.4 Innovations Need Incentives

Innovations are risky. New ideas need time and experimentation to develop, and if the idea fails, the individual has a negative return on his or her investment. So, in societies with few safety nets, innovation may be constrained. Policy can give a push to individual innovators by providing fall-back options. Risk management instruments, for example, can provide security to innovators so that they may expend resources on their new activities.

The poorest innovators need social safety nets to ensure that their families survive if the innovations fail. Since the greatest cost to these innovators is the time they spend on developing an innovation, general social safety nets insure against this income loss.

Those farther from the poverty line may need incentives to invest in innovation rather than more secure income generation activities. Innovation funds that provide grants to individuals to develop creative ideas are becoming more common. And for innovators across the poverty spectrum, policies that ensure a monopoly of returns from marketable innovations—patents, copyright laws—lower the income risk associated with developing non-rival ideas. While such legislation is outside the human development arena, its fair implementation and monitoring is crucial as individuals move through the process of implementing their ideas.

Incentives have long been used as a tool to encourage innovation in the developed world. Grand Challenges for instance, have a long history, dating all the way back to the 1700s, when the British Crown announced a *Grand Prize* for finding a way to measure longitude. In recent times, Grand Challenges have been on the rise after the Ansari X-Prize, which called for innovation in spaceflight, was introduced in the US in 1996. In 2014, the British Government announced Grand Challenges—to promote innovation in science and technology. More recently, in China, state-backed groups and institutes use the challenge-approach to widen the debate on innovation and find solutions to problems. China Association of Construction Enterprise Management, for instance, gives over 100 awards annually for innovation in construction. China's Ministry of Education oversees several national competitions in areas ranging from advertising to electric design to cloud computing. The US also has several reality TV shows that focus on business plan competitions.

Innovators need financial support at an early stage to develop and test their ideas in the marketplace. Venture funds are recognised globally as the most suitable form of providing risk capital for the growth of innovative technology and breakthrough ideas. While India is amongst the top recipients in Asia for venture funds and private equity funds, these investments are so far focused on relatively large and *safer* investments. Thus, despite the growth in the venture capital industry in India and some government schemes for supporting entrepreneurs, the seed funding stage in the innovation pipeline, where amounts required may be small but risks high, is severely constricted.

An extensive innovation ecosystem requires many lateral connections, often at local levels, between producers, sellers and financiers, and the facilitating government machinery. To induce a culture of innovation in the country, there is a need to offer encouragement through awards and challenges which mobilise people to engage and respond creatively and bring focus on neglected societal challenges.

To sum up, innovations can play a very important role in the development discourse, because they can offer a new approach to a system that is currently over-burdened by the multiple demands and has limited resources at its disposal. Enhanced focus on innovations can have an impact much beyond the realm of S&T in diverse areas such as health and education delivery, governance, enterprise development and much more. Collectively, this can herald a generational change in the country and can lay out a chart for a more sustainable and inclusive growth paradigm.

Innovation requires a financial system which is supportive and inclusive and which provides the necessary risk capital to spur innovations and enterprises. Venture funds are recognized globally as the most suitable form of providing risk capital for the growth of innovative technology and breakthrough ideas.

# 12

# Strategies and Initiatives to Promote Innovations in India

---

India has declared 2010-20 as the Decade of Innovation. The Government has stressed the need to enunciate a policy to synergize science, technology and innovation and has also established the National Innovation Council (NInC).

While supporting young firms in technology and other new-age innovative sectors is important, India also needs to develop an ecosystem that encourages innovation at more mature enterprises across the industrial spectrum—across the existing manufacturing, export, and rural and social enterprise sector. This segment has the capacity to generate a large number of jobs.

India is also uniquely poised to reap the advantages provided by a nation of 125 crore connected people, with over 800 million mobile phones, and global leadership in information and communication technology (ICT) and software. This connectivity as well as ICT talent is changing the nature of processes, business, industry, governance, education and delivery systems: and our innovation thinking also has to leverage the unprecedented advantages provided by this changing landscape of connectivity and collaboration.

Government has a critical role to play in strengthening the innovation ecosystem. It must provide the enabling policy interventions, strengthen knowledge infrastructure, improve inter-institutional collaborations, provide a mechanism for funding business innovations at all levels especially small and medium scale enterprises (SMEs) and provide vision through a national level roadmap for innovations.

India has, hitherto not accorded due importance to

innovation as an instrument of policy. The national S&T enterprise must now embrace S&T led innovation as a driver for development.

**12.1 Role of Innovations**

India is the fastest growing economy in the world, but as the pace of development increases rapidly, the country faces an increasing challenge to ensure that future growth is sustainable and inclusive. Innovation can play a key role in not only driving growth and competitive advantage, but also ensuring that this development includes a larger cross section of people and is socially, economically and environmentally sustainable. Realising that innovation is the engine for national and global growth, employment, competitiveness and sharing of opportunities in the 21st century, the Government of India declared 2010-20 as the Decade of Innovation.

Innovation can fulfil needs, which are not met by conventional means and this is critical in view of the numerous challenges the country is facing in delivering services to the people, especially at the bottom of the pyramid. In this context, India needs affordable innovations that produce products and services that are affordable by people at low levels of incomes without compromising the safety, efficiency, and utility of the products. Innovations in India hence need to cast a wider net to benefit more and more people who are currently marginalized by the system. The challenge however is how to spot, attract, nurture, and encourage sparks and talent in scientific research and identify areas of national interest and gaps for promotion of basic research and improving the quality of science education.

India is in a unique position to mount a strong initiative for affordable innovations for technologies for social and public good by taking advantages of: (a) low expertise costs, (b) vast talent base and (c) residual idealism in the society. However, engagement of multiple stakeholders and creating public private partnership for promoting people-centric research is a challenge to address national goals with specific targets in a time-bound manner. While technologies for public, strategic, and social goods would require collaborative excellence, competitive excellence models for private good would come from industrial sector, as is the case in most developed countries.

India has future challenges and large unmet needs across diverse areas such as health, education, skills, agriculture, urban and rural development, energy and so on. It also has significant challenges of exclusion and inequitable access due to multiple deprivations of class, caste and gender—all of which require innovative approaches and solutions, and looking beyond the conventional way of doing things. Innovation is going to be central to providing answers to the most pressing challenges and for creating opportunity structures for sharing the benefits of the emerging knowledge economy. Affordable solutions, innovative business models or processes which ease delivery of services to citizens can enable more people to join the development process.

## 12.2 Obstacles in Innovations

**12.2.1 Lack of Incentive for Innovations:** India traditionally has not had structures and incentives in place to encourage innovation. As India's patent system is cited as relatively weak and ineffective, there is room to use competitions and prizes as tools to encourage entrepreneurship. Competitions could be used in particular to expedite rural development and social inclusion. Though this mechanism is by no means an infallible method to encourage entrepreneurship, it can help in incentive-creation for entrepreneurship in the absence of a fully functional patent system. India has a strong scientific knowledge base that should be harnessed to solve the country's most dire socio-economic problems. If India is able to successfully achieve this, the model can be replicated across the developing world. There is a strong case to use local talent to develop solutions to rural problems. Organisations like the Honey Bee Network are focused on finding and encouraging innovations stemming from rural regions. It has documented several hundreds of these over the years.

**12.2.2 Lack of Adequate Support for Early-stage Ventures:** Incubators play an important role in supporting early-stage start-ups. Typically, they provide infrastructural support, a platform for networking, management assistance, and other support services. In comparison with traditional measures used to promote industrial development, incubation is found to positively impact the economy and create jobs with much less investment.

In India, the concept of business incubation is still at a nascent and experimental stage and focussed on urban areas. Much can be done to strengthen the scale, scope, and efficiency of business incubators. One area where there is a clear need for support is in mentoring and networking.

Incubators in India have tended to operate as silos. Though they are housed within universities in some instances, they are not adequately connected to the established corporates, so their identification of needs suffers from inadequate exposure to *real world* problems. Finally, the incubators do not learn from one another's experience.

By investing dramatically in them—not just in the per incubator allocations, but also in the institutional linkages that prevent them from each operating in isolation—India can dramatically upgrade their contribution.

**12.2.3 Inadequate Access to Capital:** Access to capital is a critical ingredient for start-up success. In India, entrepreneurs struggle to obtain funding. Access to funds is even more constrained for the economically deprived and for women. Another issue is the lack of funding available at the seed funding and angel stage. The absence of corporate venture capital (CVC) firms accentuates the problem. CVCs are an important source of financing. Apart from capital, they also offer expertise, reputation and technical knowledge when they invest in start-ups that have synergies with their companies.

Debt funding is difficult to come by. Banks tend to lend

very conservatively, and demand cash flow or collateral for financing. These are two assets most young entrepreneurs do not possess.

Inadequate government funding of research and entrepreneurship is also an issue. Government-funded research can lead to technological breakthrough. A substantial set of commercialized innovations have stemmed from the work of publicly-funded research institutions and universities in the US. For instance, Google was based on an algorithm developed as part of a research project supported by the National Science Foundation. The internet and the GPS were breakthroughs by teams initially pulled together by the Defence Advanced Research Projects Agency.

Over and above the need for more capital, there is also a need to ensure that funds invested are generating impact. As with other areas of governance, there is perhaps inordinate emphasis on reaching numerical targets and too little emphasis on ensuring that funds are utilized well.

**12.2.4 Gaps in Education and Work-Readiness:** The Indian education system is perhaps among the most unprepared for the new innovation economy. India is seen as a country facing skills shortage caused by a lack of skills development and an unresponsive education system.

The biggest problem is that the Indian school system is geared towards a rigid overly prescribed curriculum and an emphasis on rote memorization. Soft skills—collaboration, interpersonal engagement, creativity and critical thinking—are ignored in favour of single-minded test preparation.

Experts say that by the time students in India reach higher education levels they lack the creativity, critical thinking skills and open-mindedness required to become successful innovators and entrepreneurs.

**12.2.5 Disabling Business Environment:** Although, India's business environment has improved a lot over the last few years, further efforts would be required for a conducive environment to attract greater corporate investments. In the World Bank's *Doing*

*Business, 2020* survey, India ranked 63rd out of 190 countries.

A pertinent issue that requires attention is the time and cost required to shut down a failing business. Even companies that have minimal assets take on average about six months to close down under the so-called "fast track" procedure. Because of the number and expense of procedures, many owners choose to keep their defunct businesses alive on paper. This is costly in the long-term.

**12.2.6 Weak Intellectual Property Rights (IPR) Regime:** India's intellectual property regime is weak, and a deterrent to innovation. This perception is largely driven by weak enforcement of intellectual property rights, rather than the laws themselves.

Experts estimate that it takes on average five to seven years to process a patent application, and in some cases even more than a decade, as compared to two years in the United States. India had 201 patent examiners in 2012-2013. This is not enough to deal with the quantity of patents. In 2005, there were 56,171 pending patent applications; this has increased to 194,000 in 2013. A weak IPR regime on patents and trademarks reduces incentives for entrepreneurs to invest in innovation and research.

The number of patents filed in India is rising, but the numbers from other countries such as China and Korea are rising exponentially. According to a World Intellectual Property Organization (WIPO) study, India's patent application numbered 1,400 while, at the same time, China filed 24,000, Japan 45,000 and the US 63,000.

India also needs a regulatory framework that favours innovation. In every field that requires licenses the laws are old and obsolete, many of which were written over 50 years ago. There is no regulatory pathway to facilitate Indian scientists and regulators working on new technologies. For example, in the case of new medicines, there is often an insistence on replicating studies done abroad which sometimes increase the cost unnecessarily.

India needs an innovation strategy. Countries like Korea, Canada, Israel are focussing on cutting-edge technologies and encouraging both private and public sector research.

**12.2.7 Archaic Labour Laws:** Labour laws are complex and cumbersome in India. Currently, there are 40 central labour laws and 160 state laws pertaining to labour. There are many overlaps in jurisdiction. The Industrial Disputes Act is particularly rigid as it requires that companies employing more than 100 workers obtain government permission to fire a worker or close down a plant. Inflexible labour laws are a deterrent to doing business in India, and serve as a disadvantage versus South-East Asian countries.

**12.2.8 Infrastructure Bottlenecks:** India's well-documented infrastructure deficit creates barriers for entrepreneurship. While 21st century start-ups are not often associated with brick-and-mortar, they require infrastructure—roads, rails, and internet—that join them to their markets. Amongst the most significant issues are connectivity, low bandwidth availability, and the lack of electricity in cities and towns outside of major metro areas or satellite towns Typically, businesses have to incur additional costs to overcome these infrastructure deficits.

For instance, frequent power outages need to be countered by investment in expensive diesel-powered electric generators to run manufacturing units, factories, shops and even offices. Land acquisition is a notoriously time-consuming and costly process, and makes it difficult for new companies to set up businesses in India, and existing companies to physically expand their operations. Rural micro enterprises find it costly and sometimes impossible to transport their goods to more urban areas, due to poor physical infrastructure.

**12.2.9 Cultural Affinity for Stability:** The prevailing culture in middle-class India emphasizes stability and job security over risk-taking. Students have been conditioned to pursue high status and well-paid positions with reputable national and multi-national corporations as these are the main indicators of success. The salary and stability of such jobs are perceived as critical for young professionals preparing for marriage and older professionals who are beginning to consider the costs of caring for elderly or retired parents. Therefore, young workers or students prefer not to turn to the risky and financially uncertain world of entrepreneurship. The prevailing culture in the country tends to stigmatize failure.

There are sections of Indian society—like Gujaratis, Marwaris, and Parsis—that are culturally disposed to entrepreneurship. Many business families within these communities have built businesses that span the globe.

**12.2.10 Loss of Top Talent to Other Countries (or Talent Export):** Top talent from India has traditionally sought overseas opportunities, both for education and jobs. India needs to devise mechanisms to leverage its Diaspora to enhance knowledge inflows and attract talented Indians working abroad. This is especially important as return migration is often concentrated among the most successful and highly educated migrants. Recent optimism surrounding India's growth prospects has brought back some highly skilled talent to the country, but not in big enough numbers to create impact. Bringing about reverse migration will be a long-term theme as it involves offering would-be returnees not only attractive opportunities and pay, but also a western-style lifestyle. Significant effort will be required to improve urban infrastructure (roads, transportation, education), and the perceived *liveability* of cities.

**12.2.11 Trust Deficit between the Government and Private Sector:** Business and government have to work hand-in-hand to deliver economic growth and employment. Unfortunately in India, a culture of mistrust between the public and private sector has developed due to years of non-cooperation. Corporates complain of a general sense of apathy and untimeliness in law enforcement, aversion to change within the bureaucracy, the culture of rent-seeking at several layers of governance, and an erratic and mercurial political context. For instance, sectors like real-estate, defence, and manufacturing require a multitude of licenses, adding to unnecessary cost and time to complete. The licensing department has no incentive to simplify procedures as the opaque requirements allows for graft. Business leaders often complain of a slow and inefficient bureaucracy, which leads to delays in decision-making and implementation. This serves as a deterrent to public-private partnerships.

On their part, policymakers and bureaucrats complain that even meeting with senior executives from big corporate houses bring forth allegations of corruption and crony capitalism. Hence, despite their desire to help, officials are wary of being seen as partial to business, lest they be accused of wrongdoing. This fear has assumed such proportions that senior business leaders in India now complain of a total lack of engagement with policymakers. A lack of collaboration between industry and the government is damaging for investment and growth. This relationship must change to one of cooperation and collaboration to achieve mutually beneficial goals.

## 12.3 Strategies to Promote Innovations

In India, innovation is particularly needed to expedite the sluggish rural development process. Majority of India's population lives on the fringes of economic development, mired in deep-rooted multi-generational poverty. They are most vulnerable to the lack of good infrastructure, electricity, clean water, quality healthcare, and education; even as problems related to rapid development, like waste disposal and pollution continue to rise. While scientific innovation and technology offer solutions to many of the problems plaguing India and much of the developing world, these solutions are often unaffordable to the citizen or the government.

**12.3.1 Improving the Efficiency of Incubators:** Some progress has been made in developing the business incubation industry in India. Since the late 1980s, the National Science and Technology Entrepreneurship Development Board

(NSTEDB), under the Department of Science and Technology, has invested massive funds in incubators across the country. Privately-owned incubators have recently emerged, located mostly in tier-1 cities like Bangalore and Mumbai. The Start-up Village in Kerala, which won a national award for technology and business incubation in 2014, is the country's first PPP (public-private-partnership) technology incubator. However, this is not enough.

Much more can be done to improve the efficiency and scope of incubators. Firstly, more funds need to be channelled into incubators. The total value of investments in incubators remains miniscule in relation to demand.

**12.3.2 Reforming the Education System and Up-skilling Workers:** The creation of the Ministry of Skill Development and Entrepreneurship is a welcome initiative and the National Policy for Skill Development and Entrepreneurship 2015 has many excellent recommendations.

**12.3.3 Reforming School Curricula and Examination Methodology:** The curricula and examination format of the Indian central and state boards need to be overhauled and reoriented from rote-based to application-based learning and testing. The focus should be on testing higher-order skills like reasoning, analysis, lateral thinking, creativity, and judgement, rather than memorization alone. Until testing standards change, teaching and learning methods are unlikely to change.

Teaching methods that use real world problems to explain concepts and theories should be encouraged. Students should be exposed to broad needs of society—health, education, hygiene and cultural development—to promote business and entrepreneurial solutions to public policy issues.

**12.3.4 Enhanced Enforcement:** Intellectual property laws in India are compliant with Trade-Related Aspects of Intellectual Property Rights (TRIPS) administered by the World Trade Organization (WTO). However, the laws are poorly enforced, as innovation and protection of intellectual property are not prioritised adequately by enforcement officials. An important first step is spreading awareness and sensitising all the relevant authorities involved in enforcing laws, including the police and the judiciary. Further, specialised training must be provided to members of the judiciary on intellectual property and innovation, given the complexity of the cases involved.

**12.3.5 Encouraging and Recognizing Social Enterprise:** Social entrepreneurship is the recognition of a social problem and the uses of entrepreneurial principles to organize create and manage a social venture to achieve a desired social change. Social entrepreneurs are commonly associated with the voluntary and not-for-profit sectors, but this need not preclude making a profit. Social entrepreneurship has progressed significantly in India in recent years. Companies like Narayan Hospitals, Arvind Eye Hospitals, and Vaatsalya Healthcare are well-known and recognized for improving access to affordable healthcare. Pratham and Aakanksha are well-recognized for improving access to education amongst the underprivileged. Several enterprises have been set up to deliver high-quality affordable solar solutions for families living off-grid. Of late, many SMEs have been set up to encourage rural craftsmanship.

**12.3.6 Changing Cultural Attitudes:** Attitude towards entrepreneurship is likely to be a long-term exercise, and may require generational change. Recognizing that change needs to occur is an important first step for cultural attitudes to be modified. As the first generation in many families will soon be educated and will have moved up the income ladder, they may be more open to the idea of their children being self-employed. A revamp of the school system and curriculum could also play a role in encouraging entrepreneurship in the generations to come. There are some sections of Indian society (Gujaratis, Parsis, and Marwaris, for instance) which are culturally more disposed to entrepreneurship than others.

One way to expedite the entrepreneurship agenda could be to conduct exchange programmes wherein the youth from some parts of the country spend time learning in another, and vice-versa. Europe has a well-formed such exchange programme to facilitate cross-country learning, termed the *Erasmus programme*. Changing the culture of apathy, corruption, and scepticism towards intellectual property rights within the bureaucracy is also likely to take time. Consistent trust-building over time can help address the general sense of mistrust between the corporate sector and the government. The government's commitment to avoid retrospective changes in law going forward is a positive first step.

**12.3.7 Culture of Coordination and Collaboration:** Working in silos has an insidious effect on the innovation ecosystem. While there are many noteworthy entrepreneurship and innovation-boosting initiatives emerging from different sections of the government, private and non-profit sectors, the lack of coordination does not help these programmes scale and create long-lasting, long-term impact. A culture of co-ordination between ministries, departments, incubator cells across the country, enterprises, and more should be strongly encouraged and institutionalised. To monitor progress and measure impact, an annual survey of start-ups and early-stage ventures should be commissioned. The purpose of this survey should be to receive regular feedback from entrepreneurs on problem areas and areas of strength in coordination and collaboration with various stakeholders.

## 12.4 Atal Innovation Mission (AIM)

Finance Minister in his Budget Speech 2015-16 announced the Government's intention to establish the Atal Innovation Mission (AIM) in NITI Aayog and stated that initially a sum of ₹ 150 crore would be earmarked for this purpose. The overarching purpose of this mission is to promote a culture of entrepreneurship and innovation in India. In the years to come, entrepreneurship and innovation are expected to be an ever more important source of growth and job creation. New technology also has the potential to find solutions to pressing economic and social problems. AIM is seen as critical to expediting the entrepreneurial process in India.

**12.4.1 Objectives of AIM:** Key objectives of AIM are as under:

1. To create an umbrella structure to oversee innovation eco-system of the country.
2. To provide platform and collaboration opportunities for different stakeholders.
3. To study and suggest best and novel practices to be adopted by different stakeholders in the innovation chain.
4. To provide policy inputs to NITI Aayog and various Government departments and organizations.
5. To create awareness and provide knowledge inputs in creating innovation challenges and funding mechanism to government.
6. To develop new programmes and policies for fostering innovation in different sectors of economy.

**12.4.2 Role and Scope of AIM:** AIM is a catalyst for change and the vehicle that will steer the construction of a new and strong innovation ecosystem in India. Objectives of AIM conceive a self-sustaining organisation that will play the following key roles:

1. Facilitate growth and development of an innovation eco-system through policy advocacy and, in select cases, offer active implementation support.
2. Identify, recognize and reward innovations with demonstrated or clearly visible potential and impact.
3. Innovations can be of technology, business model, commercialization, working innovation, scaling-up or any other type.
4. Provide support for scaling up of solutions based on proven and promising innovations.
5. Institutional collaboration/support, tie-ups with global institutions, funding, (direct funding, or fund of funds model), other resources/support, support of policy for innovation success.
6. Identify problems of national importance, and facilitate

innovation focus by orchestrating institutional priorities, funding and other levers.
7. Establish itself as an apex governance body regarding co-ordination of innovation agenda being executed through different elements of the eco-system.
8. Authority to measuring outputs and value of innovation (without changing reporting).
9. Facilitator of internal collaboration and tie-ups with external agencies (including public-private partnerships).
10. Must have the authority to request and receive information in a timely manner

**12.5 National Innovation Foundation (NIF)**

NIF is an autonomous body of the Department of Science and Technology, Government of India. Set up in March 2000 in Ahmedabad, NIF is India's national initiative to strengthen the grassroots technological innovations and outstanding traditional knowledge. Its mission is to help India become a creative and knowledge-based society by expanding policy and institutional space for grassroots technological innovators.

NIF scouts, supports and spawns grassroots innovations developed by individuals and local communities in any technological field, helping in human survival without any help from formal sector. NIF helps grassroots innovators and outstanding traditional knowledge holders get due recognition, respect and reward for their innovations. It also tries to ensure that such innovations diffuse widely through commercial and/or non-commercial channels, generating material or non-material incentives for them and others involved in the value chain.

NIF has pooled a database of over 2,25,000 technological ideas, innovations and traditional knowledge practices (not all unique, not all distinct) from over 585 districts of the country. NIF has till date recognised 816 grassroots innovators and school students at the national level in its various National Biennial Grassroots Innovation Award Functions and annual

Dr. A.P.J. Abdul Kalam Ignite Children Award functions. In collaboration with various research & development (R&D) and academic institutions, agricultural and veterinary universities and others institutions, NIF has helped in getting several hundred grassroots technologies validated and/or value added.

NIF has also set up an augmented Fabrication Laboratory (Fab Lab) with the help of Massachusetts Institute of Technology (MIT), Boston, for product development and strengthening in-house research. Likewise, for initial validation of herbal technologies, laboratory facilities at Society for Research and Initiatives for Technologies and Institutions (SRISTI) have been augmented. Pro bono arrangement with patent firms has helped NIF file over 743 patents, including eight filed in the USA and 27 Patent Co-operation Treaty (PCT) applications, on behalf of the innovators and outstanding traditional knowledge holders. Of these, 39 patents have been granted in India and five in the USA in collaboration with the HBN.

NIF has also filed applications for 38 plant varieties developed by farmers at the Protection of Plant Varieties & Farmers' Rights Authority. Of these, five have successfully been registered.

Micro Venture Innovation Fund (MVIF) at NIF, with support from Small Industries Development Bank of India (SIDBI), has provided risk capital of more than ₹ 3.84 crore to 193 projects, some of which are at different stages of incubation. Majority of these have already been closed after receiving full repayment. As of March 31, 2016, NIF has received over 950 product inquiries from 108 countries for various technologies. It has also succeeded in commercialising products across countries in six continents, apart from being successful in materialising 89 cases of technology licensing, many with the support of Grassroots Innovation Augmentation Network (GIAN).

NIF has proved that Indian innovators can match anyone in the world when it comes to solving problems creatively. They perform better than others in generating greater sustainable alternatives by using local resources frugally. Those who see poor only as the consumers of cheap goods, miss the richness of knowledge at grassroots level and their potential as provider of ideas and innovations. The grassroots to global (G2G) model that NIF is propagating is all set to change the way the world looks at creativity and innovations at/from grassroots.

The primary objectives of NIF are as under:

1. To help India become innovative and creative, and to become a global leader in sustainable technologies by scouting, spawning and sustaining grassroots innovations.
2. To ensure evolution and diffusion of green grassroots innovation on a selective, time-bound and mission-oriented basis so as to meet the socio-economic and environmental needs of our society.
3. To provide institutional support in scouting, spawning, sustaining and scaling up grassroots green innovations as well as outstanding traditional knowledge and helping their transition to self-supporting activities.
4. To seek self-reliance through competitive advantage of innovation-based enterprises and/or application of "people-generated sustainable technologies" at grassroots level.
5. To build linkage between excellence in formal scientific systems and informal knowledge systems and create a knowledge network to link various stakeholders through application of information technology (IT) and other means.
6. To promote wider social awareness and possible applications of the know-how generated as a result of these initiatives in commercial or social spheres and encourage its incorporation in educational curriculum, developmental policies and programs.

**12.6 National Innovation Council (NInC):** It is the think-tank council of India to discuss, analyse and help implement strategies for innovation in India and suggest a Roadmap for Innovation 2010-2020.

**12.6.1 Innovation in Education**: Recognizing the fundamental role of education in nurturing and fostering an ecosystem of innovation, NInC also took a series of initiatives to encourage innovations in existing educational Institutions, as well as promoting new educational models and innovative platforms for knowledge creation, dissemination and application. Some of the key proposals of the NInc in this domain include:

1. Creation of a separate scholarship stream of National Innovation Scholarships analogous to the National Talent Search Scheme.
2. Setting up an Innovation Centre in each DIET (District Institute of Education and Training) to enhance teacher training and enable them to become facilitators of creativity and innovative thinking.
3. Mapping of Local History, Ecology and Cultural Heritage by High School students to create critical thinking on their local environment.
4. Creation of a National Innovation Promotion Service to replace/add to National Service Scheme in Colleges to use college students to identify local innovations.
5. Setting up a Meta University, as a new model for a 21st Century University to offer students a collaborative and multidisciplinary learning experience.
6. Setting up twenty Design Innovation Centres co-located in institutes of National importance.
7. Setting up of 20 University Innovation Clusters across the country where innovation would be seeded through Cluster Innovation Centres.
8. Igniting Youth Innovation with Tod Fod Jod Centers at Schools and Colleges to foster Innovation at an early stage and to create an innovative mindset in the youth.

**12.6.2 Sectoral Innovation Councils**: In order to drive innovative strategies in key sectors and create multiple roadmaps, the NInC encouraged the creation of multiple Sectoral Innovation Councils aligned to Union Government Ministries for enhancing innovation capabilities in respective sectors. The Sectoral Innovation Councils are expected to drive the innovation agenda in the country across various sectors and harness the core competencies, local talent, resources and capabilities to create new opportunities taking into consideration cross-cutting themes that impact the sector and work collaboratively with other Councils. The focus is on undertaking activities that improve the innovation quotient of the sector going forward, with a special emphasis on inclusive and sustainable innovation.

In all, 26 Ministries have constituted the Sectoral Innovation Councils. Out of these, Innovation Roadmaps have been submitted by 8 Ministries/Departments.

**12.6.3 State Innovation Councils (SInC)**: Further, NInC has also encouraged the creation of State Innovation Councils (SInCs) to replicate the efforts of the National Innovation Council to nurture an innovation ecosystem at the State level. The innovation ecosystem consists of five critical ingredients namely: (a) providing a conducive policy framework; (b) offering institutional platforms for inter-agency collaborations; (c) strengthening and expanding ICT connectivity; (d) fostering innovations in the education system; and (e) setting up a regime of incentives and rewards to encourage innovations. The SInCs are expected to carry forward the innovation movement on all these five fronts and present a Roadmap or Innovation Action Plan (IAP) for the State.

So far, 28 States and UTs have constituted the SInCs. Most of the State Governments which have formulated the Councils have focused on the multi sectoral nature of these platforms and anchored them in the Planning Departments of the State Governments, with the Departments of Science and Technology and Education as the nodal pivots to support the campaign. The focus of most of the Councils has been on areas such as Planning, S&T, Education (both School, and Higher education including Technical education), Industry, Agriculture, Rural Development, Urban Development and Information Technology.

The National Innovation Council's initiative to set up multiple innovation Councils, both at the State and sectoral level, was a first of its kind Government effort is to galvanize a large constituency around the idea of innovation. The Councils have been tasked to recommend strategies and policies for driving innovation and create an innovation movement by expanding the discourse on innovation and empowering domain experts across areas. The State Innovation Councils are also expected to sensitize State Governments to the idea of innovation and to ensure that innovation becomes a focus area in the long term development agenda of the States. Some State and Union Territory Innovation Councils have taken impressive initiatives.

**12.7 India Inclusive Innovation Fund (IIIF)**

The National Innovation Council (NInC) and the Ministry of Micro, Small and Medium Enterprises (MSME) jointly announced the creation of IIIF in January 2014. Approved by the Union Cabinet, the fund is conceived as a unique concept that seeks to combine innovation and the dynamism of enterprise to solve the problems of citizens at the base of the economic pyramid in India.

The needs of the people at the base of the economic pyramid are today served by philanthropy and government grants and subsidies, which can never be either adequate or scalable. IIIF seeks to leverage the model of venture capital to transform the lives of the less privileged.

IIIF seeks to create a new class of capital which helps set up and scale entrepreneurial skills and innovation. The fund will invest in innovative ventures that are scalable, sustainable and therefore profitable, but address social needs of the less privileged citizens in areas such as healthcare, food, nutrition, agriculture, education and skill development, energy, financial inclusion, water, sanitation employment generation, etc.

The fund is registered under SEBI's Alternative Investment Fund Category I guidelines with an initial corpus of ₹ 500 crore, with the Ministry of MSME committing to 20 percent (₹ 100 crore) and the balance being given by banks, insurance companies and overseas financial and development institutions.

The fund's eventual aim is to expand the corpus to ₹ 5,000 crore over the next 24 months. Lack of capital has been one of the major reasons why ventures and entrepreneurs seeking to address the needs at the base of the economic pyramid have failed to take off, with IIIF seeking to address exactly this gap. At least 50 percent of its investments initially would be to enterprises that fall in the MSME stage.

The IIIF would also partner the entire ecosystem in this space, including incubators, angel groups, and also public research and development programmes and laboratories to support the commercialisation and deployment of socially relevant innovative technologies and solutions. The Government would not be involved in the day to day operations of the fund, and it would be entrusted to an Asset Management Company.

# 13

# Innovation Indexes and India

## 13.1 Global Innovation Index (GII)

GII is published annually since 2007 by World Intellectual Property Organization (WIPO). [1] GII report is compiled by WIPO, Cornell University and other GII knowledge partners. The core of the GII Report consists of a ranking of world economies' innovation capabilities and results. Recognizing the key role of innovation as a driver of economic growth and prosperity, and the need for a broad vision of innovation applicable to developed and emerging economies, the GII includes indicators that go beyond the traditional measures of innovation, such as the level of research and development.

GII is a detailed quantitative tool that helps global decision makers better understand how to stimulate the innovative activity that drives economic and human development. GII is a leading benchmarking tool for business executives, policy makers and others seeking insight into the state of innovation around the world. Policymakers, business leaders and other stakeholders use the GII to evaluate progress on a continual basis.

The twelfth edition of Global Innovation Index was released in July 2019. It ranked 129 economies based on 80 indicators, ranging from intellectual property filing rates to mobile-application creation, education spending and scientific and technical publications. Its 80 indicators explore a broad vision of innovation, including political environment, education, infrastructure and business sophistication.

GII, 2018 analyzed the energy innovation landscape of the next decade and identified possible breakthroughs in fields such as energy production, storage, distribution, and consumption. It also looked at how breakthrough innovation occurs at the grassroots level and described how small-scale renewable systems are on the rise. The theme for 2019 was "Creating Healthy Lives: The Future of Medical Innovation".

India, which was ranked 81 in 2015, has steadily improved its ranking in the last four years. It went up to 66th spot in 2016, 60th in 2017, 57th in 2018 and 52nd in 2019. Thus, India jumped 29 notches in four years. The 2019 rankings put China at 14th place and Pakistan at 105 (Table 13.1).

**Table 13.1: Global Innovation Index Rankings, 2019**
**Top 10 Countries of the World and**
**China, India and Pakistan**

| Country | Rank | Score (0-100) |
|---|---|---|
| **Top Ten Countries of the World** | | |
| Switzerland | 1 (1) | 67.24 |
| Sweden | 2 (3) | 63.65 |
| United States of America | 3 (6) | 61.73 |
| Netherlands | 4 (2) | 61.44 |
| United Kingdom | 5 (4) | 61.30 |
| Finland | 6 (7) | 59.83 |
| Denmark | 7 (8) | 58.44 |
| Singapore | 8 (5) | 58.37 |
| Germany | 9 (9) | 58.19 |
| Israel | 10 (.)* | 57.43 |
| **India and its Neighbours** | | |
| China | 14 (17) | 54.82 |
| India | 52 (57) | 36.58 |
| Pakistan | 105 (109) | 25.36 |

Figures in parentheses indicate ranking of the country concerned in 2018.

* Not in top 10 in 2018.

Source: United Nations, World Intellectual Property Organization (WIPO), *Global Innovation Index, 2019.*

## 13.2 Bloomberg Innovation Index, 2019

Bloomberg is a New York-based media firm. Bloomberg's

annual innovation index, now in its seventh year, is framed using dozens of criteria including manufacturing ability, concentration of high technology public organizations, and expenditure on research and development.

The ranking for 2019 was commenced with the involvement of 200 nations. Each was scored on a 0-100 scale. Countries which did not report data were eliminated, trimming the total list to 95. Bloomberg published data for top 60 countries. Top 10 countries plus China and India are shown in Table 13.2.

**Table 13.2: Bloomberg Innovation Index Rankings, 2019**
**Top 10 Countries plus China and India**

| Rank | Country | Rank | Country |
|---|---|---|---|
| 1 (1) | South Korea | 7 (2) | Sweden |
| 2 (4) | Germany | 8 (11) | USA |
| 3 (7) | Finland | 9 (6) | Japan |
| 4 (5) | Switzerland | 10 (9) | France |
| 5 (10) | Israel | 16 (19) | China |
| 6 (3) | Singapore | 54 (debut)* | India |

Figures in parentheses show ranks in 2018.
* India entered the list of top 60 countries for the first time.

**13.2.1 Highlights of the Index:** These are as under:

1. South Korea is the most innovative country of 2019.
2. USA grabbed the 8th position.
3. China bagged the 16th position in the annual ranking.
4. United Kingdom fell to 18th position losing two spots to China.
5. World's largest emerging economies including India, Mexico, Saudi Arabia, and Vietnam also made their debut in the annual index.
6. South Africa solely represented Sub-Saharan nation in the listing.

## 13.3 NITI Aayog, India Innovation Index, 2019

NITI Aayog's first ever *India Innovation Index, 2019*

was released on October 17, 2019. NITI Aayog, along with the Institute for Competitiveness, released the report with the objective of providing a comprehensive overview of the innovation ecosystem of different administrative units of the country. The index was calculated as the average of scores of its two dimensions: enablers and performance. The report defined the following 5 enablers which act as inputs to the innovation environment: (a) human capital, (b) investment, (c) knowledge employment, (d) business environment and (e) safety and legal environment. The 2 performance pillars are: (a) knowledge output and (b) knowledge diffusion.

The index showed that the innovation ecosystem is strong in southern and western India. Delhi and Haryana are exceptions to this trend.

Karnataka emerged as the most innovative major state in India followed by Tamil Nadu, Maharashtra, Telangana, Haryana and others.

Sikkim took the top spot among North-Eastern and Hill states. Delhi was placed at the top spot among Union Territories, city and small states (Table 13.3).

**Table 13.3: India Innovation Index: State Level Performance**

| **Major States** | **Rank** | **Score** |
|---|---|---|
| Karnataka | 1 | 35.65 |
| Tamil Nadu | 2 | 32.98 |
| Maharashtra | 3 | 29.93 |
| Telengana | 4 | 22.06 |
| Haryana | 5 | 20.55 |
| Kerala | 6 | 19.58 |
| Uttar Pradesh | 7 | 19.08 |
| West Bengal | 8 | 18.21 |
| Gujarat | 9 | 16.86 |
| Andhra Pradesh | 10 | 14.51 |
| Punjab | 11 | 13.67 |
| Odisha | 12 | 12.66 |

*contd...*

| | | |
|---|---|---|
| Rajasthan | 13 | 11.00 |
| Madhya Pradesh | 14 | 9.70 |
| Chhattisgarh | 15 | 8.06 |
| Bihar | 16 | 7.99 |
| Jharkhand | 17 | 6.20 |
| **North-East and Hill States** | | |
| Sikkim | 1 | 15.49 |
| Himachal Pradesh | 2 | 13.76 |
| Uttarakhand | 3 | 13.12 |
| Manipur | 4 | 11.69 |
| Jammu & Kashmir | 5 | 11.07 |
| Tripura | 6 | 8.54 |
| Arunachal Pradesh | 7 | 8.50 |
| Assam | 8 | 7.74 |
| Nagaland | 9 | 7.49 |
| Mizoram | 10 | 6.88 |
| Meghalaya | 11 | 6.38 |
| **UTs/City States/Small States** | | |
| Delhi | 1 | 42.98 |
| Chandigarh | 2 | 27.97 |
| Goa | 3 | 22.49 |
| Puducherry | 4 | 13.94 |
| A&N Islands | 5 | 12.75 |
| Daman and Diu | 6 | 12.10 |
| Dadra and Nagar Haveli | 7 | 11.74 |
| Lakshadweep | 8 | 8.35 |

Source: NITI Aayog, *India Innovation Index, 2019*.

To sum up, currently there are many enterprises across the country which are delivering benefits to citizens and meeting the challenges of inclusion in areas such as health, education, energy, low-cost housing, sanitation, and more through innovative solutions. Often these go beyond the formal confines of R&D labs to include innovations in public service delivery or organisational innovations in local communities aimed at inclusion.

However, there is no aggregated platform or single repository to collate and disseminate these best practices and ideas. Also, while some such innovations manage to garner attention on a national scale, most of these workable solutions remain confined to their local contexts and do not achieve economies of scale because of the lack of a single platform for sharing these best practices among multiple stakeholders. Strengthening the innovation system requires a platform for information sharing and dissemination to ensure improved access to knowledge and support in the form of resources, linkages, mentoring and outreach. Greater knowledge of innovations can stimulate their adoptions and adaptations on a large scale

Government policy that favours innovation can have significant impact on growth and job creation in the economy, as indicated by economists that show innovation and productivity to be endogenously generated. Furthermore, India has a latent science and engineering talent pool, which may be particularly advantageous. This strength should be capitalised to generate indigenous intellectual capital.

**Endnote**

1. World Intellectual Property Organization (WIPO) is the global forum for intellectual property (IP) policy, services, information and cooperation. A specialized agency of the United Nations, WIPO assists its 191 member states in developing a balanced international IP legal framework to meet society's evolving needs. It provides business services for obtaining IP rights in multiple countries and resolving disputes. It delivers capacity-building programs to help developing countries benefit from using IP. And it provides free access to unique knowledge banks of IP information.

# Part III
# Entrepreneurship Development

# 14

# Entrepreneurship in India during British Rule

## 14.1 Early History of Entrepreneurial Class in India

The European travellers have testified that Indian merchants were as shrewd that they possessed in plenty business acumen and judgment and that they were not inferior in any respect to their Western counterparts including the Jews. These men, while clinging to religious rituals in their personal lives, either deviated from the spirit of their faiths or interpreted them anew to suit their business practices and activities.

Whereas the behaviour of the mercantile communities was not very entrepreneurial in the modern sense, the non-mercantile communities did not break the occupational barriers as imposed by the caste system sanctified in the scriptures. Environmental changes in a society may force re-interpretations and re-adaptations of religious and cultural beliefs.

To begin with, after making money in trade, labour contracts and financing tea and indigo plantations, the Europeans ventured into industry, like Bird and Company, Andrews Yule, Binny and Company, etc. to name a few. Rarely did tea or indigo planters or persons running specialized industries grew into big industrial owners. Only those who had business wide-ranging or an extensive government patronage could become such. Managing agency houses were real entrepreneurs in India. They adopted new methods of production, sought new sources of raw material, introduced new products and ventured into new markets. The European Managing agencies were involved in trading, agency, industry and financing.

Thus, there was hardly much distinction between

commercial and industrial interests. Whereas the Indian managing agencies which gradually grew into large industrial firms, though involved in other fields of business, in due course, were oriented more towards industrial activity. For example, the Tatas were to a greater degree involved in industrial pursuits than other kinds of businesses.

Describing the nature of entrepreneurial activities of the time, Indian Industrial Commission, 1916-18 observed, “Traders, employers and financiers differ very widely throughout the country in efficiency and the degree of success which they attain. This must be ascribed to the fact that, in the absence of proper system of industrial education and a considered policy of encouragement to industries, hereditary predisposition and the influence of surroundings have been left to produce their inevitable effect. The castes which exhibit the highest degree of intelligence are, with few exceptions, those whose functional characteristics have in the past been religious leadership, government service, or trade, and it is from these that the leading Indian industrialists, financiers and merchants have hitherto been mostly drawn. Though the representatives of these classes have attained a high degree of success in Bombay and Gujarat, and though there are numerous instances of successful Indian industrial enterprise in other parts of the country, Indian capitalists generally have followed their ancestral tradition of rural trade, and have confined themselves to the finance of agriculture and of such industries as already existed”. [1]

The British occupation of Bengal facilitated the operations of British free merchants and the entry of the company's servants into mercantile activities. Their methods were dubious, exploitative, and arbitrary. However, there is no doubt that the British displayed greater aggressiveness, drive and imagination in their business tactics, because the British environment in which they had grown up had endowed them with a superior entrepreneurial initiative.

The agency houses were established in the presidency

cities of Calcutta, Bombay and Madras during the last decades of the 18th century as supportive of British firms in London. The original purpose of these establishments was to facilitate remittances of money to Britain by Englishmen residing in India. However, since this in itself would yield little profit, these houses entered trade and commerce and added European banking and steam shipping. The number of such houses increased and their activities expanded after the East India Company lost its monopoly of the India trade in 1813. In the wake of the Industrial Revolution in Britain in the middle of the 18th century, the agency houses and the free merchants opened up new vistas for business by indicating that India had vast untapped natural resources waiting for exploitation. They financed and promoted indigo plantations, participated in the risky business of coal mining, established leather manufacturing and steel making.

The impact of colonialism was multifaceted. It provided a channel for entrepreneurs in colonies to acquire international knowledge and access international markets, although within a context of institutional racism.

### 14.2 Role of Ethnic Minorities

Entrepreneurship flourished among ethnic minorities which formed special links with colonial authorities, such as the Parsees in 19th century India. Entrepreneurial activity was mainly confined to particular communities, which were restricted by caste belongingness. The factors that enabled the entrepreneurs to carry on their businesses included intuition and the ability to utilized the opportunities. They were termed as *political merchants* in view of their connection with the colonialists.

It has been recorded that Virji Vora, the 17th century merchant prince of Surat, Gujarat had enormous liquid capital and dealt in goods of various descriptions. His mercantile operations were spread far and wide. Whenever the English East India Company needed loans, it approached Vora who would gladly advance funds at exorbitant rates of interest. His position in the market was unassailable, but there is nothing to suggest that the enormous profits he earned were utilized either for diversification or manufacturing.

There were other ethnic businessmen who displayed their entrepreneurial skills.

**14.2.1 Bengalis:** Bengalis had come in contact with the British perhaps much earlier than the Parsees did. Interestingly, till quite late into the 20th century, the Bengalis kept themselves aloof from trade and industry. It is generally held that the predominant section of the Bengalis (the middle classes) looked down upon trade and industry and preferred to be professionals. Also the long gestation period of industry did not promise quick returns, so the Bengali Businessman felt satisfied with trading. Moreover, the big merchants of Eastern India having invested their money in becoming landlords were thus eliminated by the Permanent Settlement from venturing into industry.

The Jagat Seths, who flourished in the early half of the 18th century in the eastern part of India, depended mainly on money lending and amassed a huge wealth. They supported the English in their economic and political activities and were a decisive factor in the turn of events which gave Bengal to the British in 1757. The Seths were the collectors of revenue to the Nawab of Bengal during the pre-Plassey days. They lent their support to the British probably without realizing that the emergence of the British as a territorial power would end their main source of profit. Thus, the traditional mercantile classes dominated the business and commercial activities almost till the onset of the 19th century but they introduced no qualitative change in the business practices of their forefathers and that they remained wedded to liquidity preference. There is no evidence to suggest that occupational division, sanctioned by the caste system, underwent any change.

Bengal had produced outstanding persons like Dwarka Nath Tagore who organized the Union Bank in association with the European Merchants. He became the pioneer in many fields like industry and steam navigation on the rivers of India. He had great liking for Western ideas and culture. After the fall of the agency houses in Bengal, as a result of the depression of 1829, Dwarkanath proceeded to fill the vacuum. He founded the Carr Tagore Company jointly with William Carr to participate in the same kind of activities which had remained in the hands of the agency houses. He established a bank, a steamship company and a colliery and promoted a host of minor ventures. Dwarkanath belonged to a big landlord family and it is possible that the permanent settlement, introduced in Bengal during the closing decades of the 18th century, had improved his financial position and so enabled him to promote his business ventures.

Dwarkanath and a few of his associates made some attempts to form the Bengal Tea Association, but uncertain about the future they gladly stepped aside when some Englishmen established the Assam Company in 1838 in London to exploit the tea resources of Assam.

After the death of Dwarka Nath, there was a virtual lull in individual activity among the Bengalis with the entire Bengal and the adjoining areas converted into a massive farm-yard to meet the requirements for Britain's exports and raw materials for mass production consumer industries.

Between 1834 and 1847, a host of partnership ventures were started jointly by Bengalis and Englishmen. Those who participated in these ventures were ideologically and culturally close to the English either by personal contacts or by education. Probably safe in their traditional lines of money-lending and trade, the traditional business classes, with little contacts with new values, refrained from entering the more challenging fields. The partnerships remained confined to the lines made relatively familiar by the agency houses or free merchants.

Murshidabad had many silk centres and it was a major East India Company commercial centre that Lord Clive compared the town to London.

**14.2.2 Parsees:** Journey of Indian industries began with cotton textile. The first cotton mill was established in the year 1854 by a member of the Parsee community, a successful cotton merchant of that time.

Parsees were able to create the Tata business combine, though there were no comparable Hindu business combines. Indeed, the Parsees grew into the richest group of entrepreneurs in India through their participation in opium and yarn trade with China and were able to control Bombay business by the mid-19th century, which enabled them to develop into leading industrial combine.

Parsees came into early prominence to compete with European businessmen and gain a sizeable share of control in trade and industry. Some are of the view that they possessed protestant-like ethical value-system which enabled them to be prosperous. Possession of enterprising qualities was intrinsic for the Parsees as a community.

Giving due importance to the special qualities of the Parsees, however, it is essential to consider the initial advantages they had because of the prevailing circumstances and their location, which played an important part in protecting them from severe competition. Parsees as a community had settled In India for nine hundred years before they took to trade. They primarily depended on land for their living. They were not bound by rules of the caste system. Besides, no gainful occupation was considered shameful by them. When the European merchants landed on the western parts of India by sea, the Parsees had no inhibition to work for them as go betweens. Coming in contact with the Europeans quite early, they got the needful exposure with the outside world which initially enabled them to be brokers, agents or interpreters for the British and Dutch merchants and later in trading with the other foreigners. When the British established the port and a factory in Bombay, many of the Parsees went and settled there. As Bombay prospered with the decline of the port in Surat, the

Parsees also prospered. They accumulated a lot of capital first from opium trade and then from cotton trade, especially during the American Civil War.

The other important factor which went in favour of Parsees, in comparison to their eastern counterparts, was that they belonged to a region which, till quite late, was not under British influence. Western India did not experience the dastardly conquests and plunders of the early British East India Company. For long, the British were resisted by the Marathas of this region. The Parsees worked alongside the British and were also financiers. During the period, they were also friends with the British. During the Indian freedom struggle they played an important role in the Bombay Presidency, both in entrepreneurship and political struggle. The hinterland of Bombay was not as extensive as that of Calcutta and before the coming of railways, western India was quite inaccessible.

The relatively arid Deccan Plateau was not favourable for plantation of tea or indigo and the region did not have rich mines like Bengal and Bihar. Thus, there was not much reason for the British to be attracted and establish themselves in Western India for a long time. Late British interference enabled not only the Parsees but all the other communities involved in trading to build up and face lesser competition from the British than their counterparts elsewhere did.

One particular Parsee enterprising family was the Wadias, who were known for shipbuilding activities. They were the suppliers to the East India Company. Lack of inhibitions to go on overseas journey probably made them more flexible in their trading activities and put them in an advantageous position to acquire technical knowledge. The Parsees were not only a conspicuous lot in industry but also out-numbered all others in the supervisory jobs in cotton mills. Their enterprise was not limited to trading and industry. They were also esteemed for their highly developed civic sense. Further, the Parsees were known for generously donating money for public causes.

Navsari (in the hinterland of Bombay) was a cotton centre

dominated by Parsees. Parsee entrepreneurs effected the substitution of traditional products by new products which were cheaper as a result of large scale production.

**14.2.3 Marwaris:** Marwaris (or banias) specialized in domestic trade. Their enterprises complemented those of English entrepreneurs and became prominent in a diversified industrial economy.

Marwari community of Calcutta controlled the economic activity of east India. They were regarded as *northern imperialists*, being shunned by the locals. Marwari group of Calcutta had developed from the merchant class of Rajaputana. After using Murshidabad as their base, they slowly penetrated into Calcutta. As they extended their influence, they came into close contact with the imperialists in both economic and political activities. However, the alien culture and profit-seeking attitude of the marwaris earned the wrath of local politicians and public.

The Birla combine of the Marwari community was characterized by solidarity of family ties and has been mainly involved in the production of consumption goods.

**14.2.4 Others:** Gujaratis of large cities were diligent and adventurous and following the example of the Parsees were venturing into new business combines. Jains had long been (and still are) a trading community.

## 14.3 Non-trading Communities as Entrepreneurs

Prior to First World War, those who tried their hand in industrial venture seldom belonged to the trading communities. However, things changed after the war. Many professionals, like doctors and lawyers, also started taking part in entrepreneurial activities. Often the landlords were also associated.

In Bengal, the National Tannery was started by Nilratan Sarkar. Dr. P.C. Roy is considered the founder of Bengal Chemical and Pharmaceutical works. Maharaja Mahindra Chandra Nandy and Baikunthanath Sen collaborated to establish the Calcutta Pottery. Sir Rajindra Nath Mukherjee on his own merit was a great entrepreneur.

In Bombay, Dr. Balchandra Bhatwadekar and Laxrnan Rao Kirloskar were known for their industrial enterprise. Kirloskar, one of the most imaginative entrepreneurs, started manufacturing agricultural machines.

In Punjab, the Electrical Supply Company Limited, the Bharat Insurance and many other companies including cotton mills were founded by Lala Harkishan Lal. A lawyer by training, he belonged to the Arora caste.

In the United Provinces the Raja of Barot had started a sugar factory.

In Ahmedabad, Ranchood Lal Chotalal, a Nagar Brahmin, established a cotton mill on modern lines. In 1847, he failed in his first attempt but again in 1851 he raised money and against all odds was able to reopen the mill in 1861.

### 14.4 Factors Responsible for Poor Entrepreneurial Initiatives

Apart from the British inhibitive industrial policies, the Indian social structure did not support the growth of entrepreneurs in the country. The caste-based traditional social structure had fixed occupation for each individual and provided very little liberty for occupational mobility.

Traditional business caste people, due to their occupational heritage and training in business activities, entered entrepreneurial arena first. Other caste people could not pace with them in this field due to their non-conducive social background. The scheduled castes had and have the lowest representation in the business field.

The rise of Indian entrepreneurial class was marked by the entry into manufacturing sector initiated by the three communities of the country: Parsees, Gujaratis and the Marwaris. These communities were initially traders and also did not occupy a clear-cut defined social position in the caste hierarchy. These communities had a background of business family. Parsees were ship-builders, Gujaratis were traders and the Marwaris had the background of money lending.

Indian society was marked by an assemblage of different castes and communities characterized by their specific social and occupational norms. These communities influenced the course of development in the country. It is because of this perhaps that the Indian entrepreneurship was numerically dominated by traditional trading castes.

Economic historians have tried to analyze the sociological conditions which played a role in entrepreneurial development in the country. Business class mostly came from the social communities that were traditionally involved in trading, finance and handicraft activities in different geographical areas.

The negative approach of the British did not allow Indian entrepreneurship to develop smoothly and satisfactorily. Though modern industrial production may be said to have begun around 1850 but two features were dominant:

1. Most of the industrial units were established by the British except a few which could be called truly Indian concerns.
2. British imposed a new economic policy in India which had the objective of converting Indian economy into a colonial market by plundering its natural resources and obstructing the development of its indigenous productive forces.

It is important to note that the British rulers invested much in the transport and communication sector though for their own economic requirements. The British industrialists built a well-knit network with the Indian business class which consisted of native importers and exporters, brokers, merchants, landlords and users.

The native capitalists helped foreign ones in consolidating their economic interests in this country. As the network grew, the peasants and village artisans became impoverished. Gradually industrial bourgeoisie developed in India from merchants and moneylenders. However, Indian bourgeoisies remained mostly trading partners than an industrial class.

The basic weakness with the Indian capitalists became

apparent at the end of the colonial rule in India. The means of production required for the development of industry were virtually absent. Except for very meagre production of iron and steel, coal and a few chemicals etc., the articles of productive consumption were hardly produced in India.

Before Independence, only the big bourgeoisie monopolized the industrial arena of the country. Significant changes have taken place in recent years in the socio-economic composition of the entrepreneurial class of India.

To sum up, modern industrial activity in India started around the middle of the 19th century. It was a very modest beginning and most of manufacturers in the beginning were the British. Cotton, jute and coal were the first fields which constituted the industrial sector. This was the time which marked the end of the dominance of the traditional industries and opening of the gate for the supply of indigenous entrepreneurship. Activities of the British entrepreneurs in India pointed to increasing business opportunities, gave the Indians a form of corporate management, brought them face-to-face with superior technology and contributed to their capacity to borrow it by ensuring the availability of personnel to handle the new machines. While the established business groups responded to the new opportunities by diversifying their activities and entering into foreign collaboration to exploit the relatively less familiar fields, others began to enter into diverse undertakings.

**Endnote**

1. *Report of the Indian Industrial Commission, 1916-18*, p. 64.

# 15

# Importance and Obstacles to Entrepreneurship Development

The growth and prosperity of all economies remains highly dependent on entrepreneurial activity. Entrepreneurs are the essence of economic growth as they provide a source of income and employment for themselves, create employment for others, produce new and innovative products or services, and drive greater upstream and downstream value-chain activities. Supportive environments are increasingly essential to successful entrepreneurship and these are evolving across the world. The ideal entrepreneurial environment has 5 pillars:

1. Access to funding.
2. Entrepreneurial culture.
3. Supportive regulatory and tax regimes.
4. Educational systems that support entrepreneurial mindsets.
5. A co-ordinated approach that links the public, private and voluntary sectors.

The face of entrepreneurship is also changing. Across the world, entrepreneurs are increasingly young and/or female due to increasing unemployment. The public and private sector each have an important role to play in creating entrepreneurial ecosystems that, in addition to funding, are essential to promoting entrepreneurial success.

Highlighting the diversity of the country, four kinds of entrepreneurial activities exist: (a) factor-driven entrepreneurship, (b) efficiency-driven entrepreneurship, (c) innovation-driven entrepreneurship and (d) necessity-driven entrepreneurship.

Developed economies generate entrepreneurial opportunities as a result of their wealth and innovation capacity, yet they also offer more wage employment options to attract those that might otherwise become independent entrepreneurs. If these opportunities for entrepreneurship and innovation are to be captured, it is essential to create an enabling eco-system for entrepreneurship to thrive and instil a mind-set and culture of opportunity and innovation-based motives and entrepreneurial incentives.

## 15.1 Who is an Entrepreneur?

An entrepreneur is an individual who organizes and operates a business or businesses, taking on financial risk to do so. The entrepreneur is commonly seen as an innovator of new ideas, and business processes. Management skill and strong team building abilities are often perceived as essential leadership attributes for successful entrepreneurs. Leadership, management ability, and team-building are considered to be the essential qualities of an entrepreneur.

Psychological studies show that the psychological propensities for male and female entrepreneurs are more similar than different. A growing body of work shows that entrepreneurial behaviour is dependent on social and economic factors. For example, countries with healthy and diversified labour markets or stronger safety nets show a more favourable ratio of opportunity-driven rather than necessity-driven women entrepreneurs. Empirical studies suggest that male entrepreneurs possess strong negotiating skills and consensus-forming abilities.

Research studies that explore the characteristics and personality traits of, and influences on, the entrepreneur have come to differing conclusions. Most, however, agree on certain consistent entrepreneurial traits and environmental influences. Although certain entrepreneurial traits are required, entrepreneurial behaviours are also dynamic and influenced by environmental factors. The entrepreneur is solely concerned with opportunity recognition and exploitation, although the opportunity that is recognised depends on the type of entrepreneur.

Some of the most significant influences on an individual's decision to become an entrepreneur are workplace peers and the social composition of the workplace.

The ability of entrepreneurs to innovate is thought to relate to innate traits such as extroversion and a proclivity for risk-taking. The capabilities of innovating, introducing new technologies, increasing efficiency and productivity, or generating new products or services, are characteristic qualities of entrepreneurs. Entrepreneurs are catalysts for economic change, and researchers argue that entrepreneurs are highly creative individuals with a tendency to imagine new solutions by finding opportunities for profit or reward. It is widely maintained that entrepreneurs are unusual individuals. In line with this view, there is an emerging research tradition investigating the genetic factors that are perceived to make entrepreneurs so distinctive.

However, there are also critical perspectives that attribute these research attitudes to oversimplified methodological and/or philosophical assumptions. For example, it has been argued that entrepreneurs are not that distinctive, but that it is in essence unrealistic preconceptions about *non-entrepreneurs* that maintain laudatory portraits of *entrepreneurs*.

## 15.2 What is Entrepreneurship?

In political economics, entrepreneurship is the quality of being an entrepreneur, i.e. one who *undertakes an enterprise*. The term puts emphasis on the risk and effort taken by individuals who both own and manage a business, and on the innovations resulting from their pursuit of economic success.

Entrepreneurship in this sense may result in new organizations or may be part of revitalizing mature organizations in response to a perceived opportunity. The most obvious form of entrepreneurship is that of starting new businesses (referred as a start-up company). In recent years, the term has been extended to include social and political forms of entrepreneurial activity. When entrepreneurship is describing activities within a firm or large organization it is referred to as intra-preneurship and may include corporate venturing, when large entities spin-off organizations.

Entrepreneurial activities are substantially different depending on the type of organization and creativity involved. Entrepreneurship ranges in scale from solo projects (even involving the entrepreneur only part-time) to major undertakings creating many job opportunities. Many high value entrepreneurial ventures seek venture capital or angel funding (seed money) in order to raise capital to build the business. Many kinds of organizations now exist to support would-be entrepreneurs including specialized government agencies, business incubators, science parks, and some NGOs. In more recent times, the term entrepreneurship has been extended to include elements not related necessarily to business formation activity such as conceptualizations of entrepreneurship as a specific mindset resulting in entrepreneurial initiatives e.g. in the form of social entrepreneurship, political entrepreneurship, or knowledge entrepreneurship have emerged.

The supposition that entrepreneurship leads to economic growth is an interpretation of the residual in endogenous growth theory and as such is hotly debated in academic economics. An alternate description suggests that the majority of innovations may be much more incremental improvements such as the replacement of paper with plastic in the construction of a drinking straw.

Entrepreneurship is about taking risk. The behaviour of the entrepreneur reflects a kind of person willing to put his or her career and financial security on the line and take risks in the name of an idea, spending much time as well as capital on an uncertain venture.

The acts of entrepreneurship are often associated with true uncertainty, particularly when it involves bringing something really novel to the world, whose market never exists.

## 15.3 Role and Importance of Entrepreneurs

Entrepreneurs play an important role in the economic development of a country. Successful entrepreneurs innovate, bring new products and concepts to the market, improve market efficiency, build wealth, create jobs, and enhance economic growth. The ability of entrepreneurs to create jobs is certainly relevant to India, given the need for incremental new jobs.

De novo firms that unleash creative destruction shift surpluses from rent-seeking large producers to consumers and broader society. Joseph Schumpeter, eminent American economist, put innovation at the heart of economic theory and capitalism. He proposed that innovation was the process by which economies were able to break out of their static mode and enter a path of dynamism. It was his theory of *creative destruction* that first highlighted the importance of innovators in revolutionizing the economic structure, leading to the creation of new products, services, and markets, and the decay of the old. Just as boosting entrepreneurship can lead to growth and job creation, failing to promote entrepreneurship can lead to stagnation, and social and economic inertia.

While India celebrates the success of several new ventures in e-commerce, information technology and mobile telephony, these are not sufficient to deliver aggregate growth expectations. The agricultural sector remains moribund, the rural economy neglected, and vast sectors starved of capital and talent, constrained as these are by collective under-investment in the requisite supporting institutions. Similar institutional inadequacy challenges bedevil investments in so-called social enterprises as well. India will have to encourage creation of new small and medium enterprises (SMEs) focused on manufacturing and innovation, while spurring rural innovation and growth. Hence, putting entrepreneurship at the forefront of the economic agenda is the need of the hour.

The ability of entrepreneurs to create jobs is particularly relevant to India given its employment crisis. India's *demographic dividend* [1] must be reaped. By 2020, 63 percent of India's population will be of working age. McKinsey estimates that India's working-age population will grow by 69 million between 2012 and 2022. Cashing in on this dividend will require India to create 69 million additional appropriate jobs, as well as jobs for those that are currently unemployed. Creation of new businesses will therefore be an important avenue for absorption of these workers. Therefore, developing and sustaining a vibrant entrepreneurial fabric is one policy option that should be part and parcel of any economic development plan.

### 15.4 Obstacles to Entrepreneurship in India

1. Lack of incentives for innovation at the national level.
2. Lack of efficient business incubators.
3. Insufficient access to capital.
4. Archaic education system.
5. Lack of work-related skills amongst the youth.
6. Disabling business environment.
7. Culture and mindset.

The biggest cultural obstacle to unleashing entrepreneurial potential is middle-class India's scepticism about entrepreneurship. Notwithstanding the exuberance around the IT sector at the moment, in the *mainstream* of the economy, there continues to be suspicion, even distaste, evinced by the idea of entrepreneurship.

Young creative individuals are often held back from starting new ventures due to inherent scepticism amongst family members. Given this cultural context, any blueprint that intends to effectively encourage entrepreneurship must promote and embrace a risk-taking and creative mindset. A related cultural obstacle to innovation is the limited tolerance for failure in Indian society. Experimentation and failure are integral parts of creating and building new ventures. Therefore, a societal tolerance for failure as part and parcel of the learning process needs to be inculcated.

Apart from the overarching theme of a generalized

aversion toward risk-taking and failure in India, other more subtle cultural impediments also present a challenge to entrepreneurship and innovation. These include: (a) general sense of apathy and untimeliness in law enforcement, (b) aversion to change within the bureaucracy, (c) culture of rent-seeking at several layers of governance, (d) cultural skepticism toward intellectual property rights and (e) general, pervasive and deeply corrosive sense of mistrust between the government and the private sector.

These factors slow down the private sector in India. Other cultural impediments include a general de-prioritization of soft skills in favour of hard technical knowledge, and a bias by employers against graduates hailing from non-elite institutions or non-engineering backgrounds, amongst others.

To sum up, the Indian capacity for harnessing entrepreneurship has not been fully realized. Given the realities of rapidly changing economic landscape in the country, entrepreneurship opportunities have emerged as an important source of meeting the aspirations of the youth. An all inclusive approach to strengthen the entrepreneurship development scenario in the country which is competent, quality conscious, market savvy, innovative and has globally competitive entrepreneurs, needs to be carefully mentored and encouraged.

Job creation for skilled youth is also a major challenge before the nation. Entrepreneurship based on innovation has immense growth potential. However, the number of local entrepreneurs emerging every year in India is very low. Accelerating entrepreneurship especially that based on innovation is crucial for large-scale employment generation in India.

Entrepreneurial culture in India is picking up. Bangalore has been listed within the world's 20 leading start-up cities in the 2015 Start-up Genome Project ranking. It is also ranked as one of the world's five fastest growing start-up cities. Nevertheless, much of this entrepreneurship is limited to IT.

To create new jobs, India must move beyond its reliance on IT achievements and the industrial conglomerates that drove earlier post-liberalization growth. For example, India needs to develop technological capabilities to serve the requirements of its core industries—capital goods used in manufacturing industries are mostly imported, as are electronic goods.

There is tremendous scope to boost entrepreneurship in India. Some sectors immediately provide opportunities for growth. Sectors like IT infrastructure, biotechnology, healthcare and education, too are poised to grow several times in size over the next couple of years. There is huge scope in the field of social inclusion. Bringing the economically disenfranchised (including scheduled castes, scheduled tribes, and other backward castes) and women into the economic mainstream not only serves a higher purpose; there is also a strong economic and social justification for the same. It would lead to greater stability in society in the years to come (a benefit across all socio-economic strata), and would also open up a significant new market for firms to tap. As such, it would substantially increase the proportion of the economy able to engage in productive activity.

**Endnote**

1. If the massive population of India is properly educated and trained, it can prove a boon for the national economy. India's demographic dividend is essentially due to two factors: (a) declining birth rates and (b) improvement in life expectancy. The declining birth rate changes the age distribution and makes for a smaller proportion of population in the dependent ages and for relatively larger share in the productive labour force. The result is low dependency ratio which can provide comparative cost advantage and competitiveness to the economy. Moreover, the global economy is expected to witness a skilled man power shortage to the extent of around 56 million by 2020. Thus, the *demographic dividend* in India needs to be exploited not only to expand the production possibility frontier but also to meet the skilled manpower requirements of India and other countries.

# 16

# Entrepreneurship Development Institutes and Schemes in India

Entrepreneurship has been considered the backbone of economic development. It has been well-established that the level of economic growth of a region, to a large extent, depends on the level of entrepreneurial activities in the region. The myth that entrepreneurs are born, no more holds good. Rather, it is well-recognised now that the entrepreneurs can be created and nurtured through appropriate interventions in the form of entrepreneurship development programmes.

In the era of liberalisation, privatisation and globalization along with ongoing IT revolution, capable entrepreneurs are making use of the opportunities emerging from the evolving scenario. However, a large segment of the population, particularly in the industrially backward regions/rural areas generally lags behind in taking advantage of these opportunities. Therefore, there is a need to provide skill development and entrepreneurship development training to such people in order to bring them to mainstream of economic growth.

## 16.1 National Level Entrepreneurship Development Institutes in India

Entrepreneurship development programmes (EDPs) are being organized as a regular training activity to cultivate the latent qualities of youth by enlightening them on various aspects that are necessary to be considered while setting up enterprises. These programmes are conducted generally for technicians/artisans for motivating them towards self-employment. The course contents of such EDPs are so designed as to provide useful information on: (a) product/process design, (b) manufacturing practices involved, (c) testing and quality control, (d) selection and usage of appropriate machinery and equipments, (e) project profile preparation, (f) marketing avenues/techniques, (g) product/service pricing, (h) export opportunities, (i) infrastructure facilities available, (j) finance and financial institutions, and (k) cash flows. No fees are charged from scheduled castes, scheduled tribes, women and physically handicapped participants in the stipendiary programmes. Rather, they are eligible for a stipend of ₹ 125 per week. Emphasis is given to special programmes in rural areas particularly for weaker sections of the society.

Similarly, entrepreneurship skill development programmes (ESDPs) are organized to upgrade existing skills and to create new skills in workers and technicians of existing units and educated unemployed youth by organizing various technical training courses for them. The basic objective has been to provide training to unskilled/semi-skilled workers engaged in MSMEs sector and to equip them with better and improved techno-managerial skills of production. Emphasis is given to organize the maximum programmes in rural areas particularly for weaker sections of the society. Specific tailor-made programmes are organized for the skill development of the socially disadvantage groups (OBCs, SCs, STs, minorities and women) in remote regions/pockets of the States. These programmes are also called *Out-Reach Programmes* as these are conducted in rural/less developed areas.

Entrepreneurship development and training is, thus, one of the key elements for development of MSMEs, particularly the first generation entrepreneurs. To undertake this task on regular basis, the Ministry of MSMEs has set up the following 3 national-level entrepreneurship development institutes (EDIs) as autonomous bodies. These institutes are engaged in: (a) developing training modules, (b) undertaking research and training and (c) providing consultancy services for entrepreneurship development and promotion of MSMEs, including enhancement of their competitiveness.

1. National Institute for Micro, Small and Medium Enterprises (NI-MSME), Hyderabad.

2. National Institute for Entrepreneurship and Small Business Development (NIESBUD), NOIDA (Uttar Pradesh).
3. Indian Institute of Entrepreneurship (IIE), Guwahati.

**16.1.1 National Institute for Micro, Small and Medium Enterprises (NIMSME), Hyderabad:** It is an organization of the Ministry of MSMEs, Government of India. NI-MSME was originally set up as Central Industrial Extension Training Institute (CIETI) in New Delhi in 1960 as a Department under the Ministry of Industry and Commerce, Government of India. It was decided to keep it free from the tardy and impeding administrative controls and procedures, so that the Institute can play a pivotal role in the promotion of small enterprise. Therefore, the Institute was shifted to Hyderabad in 1962, and was renamed as Small Industry Extension Training (SIET) Institute.

**A. Centres of Excellence:** SIET was conferred the status of national institute by the Government of India with the charter of assisting in the promotion of small enterprises mainly by creating a pro-business environment. In 1984, UNIDO recognised SIET as an institute of meritorious performance under its Centres of Excellence Scheme. Subsequently, it was also accorded the national status in the same year and SIET Institute became NI-SIET. Since then, the Institute has come a long way, carving a place of distinction for itself in the domain of entrepreneurship promotion, achieving recognition both at the national level and in the international arena. To cope with the pressure of globalisation, the Government of India enacted the MSMED Act which became effective from 2nd October 2006. Accordingly, the Institute, in order to reflect the expanded focus of its objectives with name was rechristened as NI-MSME from April 11, 2007 and re-designed its structure and organisation. It is an organisation of the Ministry of Micro, Small and Medium Enterprises.

**16.1.2 National Institute for Entrepreneurship and Small Business Development (NIESBUD), NOIDA, (Uttar Pradesh):** NIESBUD [1] is a premier institute established in 1983 for coordinating and over viewing the activities of various institutions/agencies engaged in developing entrepreneurship, primarily in small industry, small business and human resources development. NIESBUD has been actively engaged in organizing national/international training programmes, which have benefited MSMEs in India and in other countries.

**A. Objectives of NIESBUD:** These are as follows:

1. To evolve standardised materials and processes for selection, training, support and sustenance of entrepreneurs, potential and existing.
2. To help/support and affiliate institutions/organisations in carrying out training and other entrepreneurship development related activities.
3. To serve as an apex national level resource institute for accelerating the process of entrepreneurship development ensuring its impact across the country and among all strata of the society.
4. To provide vital information and support to trainers, promoters and entrepreneurs by organising research and documentation activities relevant to entrepreneurship development.
5. To train trainers, promoters and consultants in various areas of entrepreneurship development.
6. To offer consultancy nationally/internationally for promotion of entrepreneurship and small business development.
7. To provide national/international forums for interaction and exchange of experiences helpful for policy formulation and modification at various levels.
8. To share international experience and expertise in entrepreneurship development.
9. To share experience and expertise in entrepreneurship development across national frontiers.

**B. Activities of NIESBUD:**

**(a) Assisting/Supporting EDPs:**

1. Evolving standardized materials, research, and publications.
2. Formulation of standardised procedures of identification and

selection of potential entrepreneurs.

3. Preparation of training aids materials: (a) manuals, (b) handbooks, (c) lesson plans, (d) learning text, (e) case studies, and (f) EMT kits etc.

**(b) Training of Trainers/Promoters:**

1. Accreditation programme for entrepreneurial motivation trainers.
2. Trainers' training programme for enterprise launching and management.
3. Trainers/promoters programme for support organizations.
4. Small business promotion programme.
5. Entrepreneurship orientation programme for senior executives.

**(c) Research and Publications:**

1. Research on topics related to entrepreneurship and allied areas: (a) disseminates the findings widely, (b) status analysis study on entrepreneurship in India, (c) potential of women entrepreneurship in India, (d) successful women entrepreneurs, their identity, expectations and problems and (e) directory of EDP institutions in India.
2. Information materials for entrepreneurs like handbooks on industrial laws, commercial laws, ready reckoner for product selection etc.
3. Directory of experts.
4. Newsletter covering schemes, news, views, forthcoming activities, agency profile, entrepreneurial profile etc.

**(d) Creation and Capacity Building of EDP Institutions:**

The Institute provides support and guidance in establishing EDP institutions. The assistance covers developing programmes and faculty, providing training, library facilities and sharing experiences of conducting programmes at the initial stage(s).

**(e) Small Business in Focus:** The Institute focuses its attention on small business development by encouraging and supporting arrangements in remote and backward areas. The number and percentage of small business among small entrepreneurs is very large. The Institute concentrates its efforts on evolving methodology for training, supporting and sustaining this Group.

**(f) National/International Forum for Exchange of Ideas and Experiences**

1. The Institute organises National as well as international meets for sharing experiences with a view to enhance success in implementation of entrepreneurship development programmes.
2. Organises workshops and seminars on contemporary topics/issues such as sustaining entrepreneurship, emerging entrepreneurial opportunities etc.
3. Encourages foreign delegations for mutual exchange of experiences.

**(g) Developing Entrepreneurial Culture:**

1. The Institute strives to create climate conducive to emergence of entrepreneurs from all strata of society.
2. Conducts awareness campaigns for students of school and college and institutions of higher learnings.
3. Produces and distributes material for use by mass media like television etc.
4. Organises group discussions representing a variety of cross-sections of the society.

**(h) Services to Affiliate Members:** The Institute affiliates individuals/institutions/organisations engaged in entrepreneurship development and related activities such as ordinary, associate and corporate members. The Institute offers the following services to the members:

1. Discussing strategy for propagating entrepreneurship.
2. Provision of concessional facilities.
3. Free services (library, documentation etc.).
4. Free academic advice/guidance.

**(i) Sustaining Entrepreneurship:** Sustaining existing entrepreneurs is an important activity. In this direction, the Institute organises continuing education programmes for small entrepreneurs besides providing counselling and consultancy. Short duration training programmes on working capital management, marketing, project identification and selection, accounting etc. are conducted on campus while counselling/consultancy is provided on and off campus.

**16.1.3 Indian Institute of Entrepreneurship (IIE), Guwahati [2]:** With an aim to undertake training, research and consultancy activities in small and micro enterprises focusing on entrepreneurship development, IIE was established in the year 1993 in Guwahati by the erstwhile Ministry of Industry (now the Ministry of Micro, Small and Medium Enterprises), Government of India as an autonomous national institute. The Institute began operating from April 1994 with the North East Council (NEC), Governments of Assam, Arunachal Pradesh and Nagaland and SIDBI as its other stakeholders.

**A. Objectives:** Following are the objectives of IIE:

1. To organize and conduct training for entrepreneurship development.
2. To evolve strategies and methodologies for different target groups and locations and conduct field tests.
3. To identify training needs and offer training programmers to Government and non-Government organizations engaged in promoting and supporting entrepreneurship.
4. To document and disseminate information needed for policy formulation and implementation related to self-employment.
5. To identify, design and conduct training programmers for existing entrepreneurs.
6. To prepare and publish literature related to entrepreneurship and industrial development.
7. To organize seminars, workshops and confer conferences for providing a forum for interaction and exchange of views by various agencies and entrepreneurs.
8. To conduct research for generating knowledge to accelerate the process of entrepreneurship development.
9. To act as a catalyst for development of self-employment/entrepreneurship, industry/business.
10. To evolve, design and help in the utilization of various media for creating entrepreneurship.

**B. Activities:** The activities of IIE include the following:

1. Identification of training needs.
2. Designing and organizing programmes, both for development functionaries and entrepreneurs.
3. Evolving effective training strategies and methodologies for different target groups and locations.
4. Organizing seminars, workshops and conferences for providing fora for interaction and exchange of views by various agencies and entrepreneurs.
5. Undertaking research on entrepreneurship development.
6. Documenting and disseminating information needed for policy formulation and implementation on self-employment and entrepreneurship.

IIE acts as a catalyst for entrepreneurship development by creating an environment for entrepreneurship in the support system, developing new entrepreneurship, helping in the growth of existing entrepreneurs and propagation of entrepreneurial education.

Considering the importance of creating environment for entrepreneurship development, IIE has been organizing a number of programmes to create awareness about entrepreneurship. Creating awareness on entrepreneurship among the students has been one of the core areas of IIE. It organizes faculty development programmes for university and college teachers and awareness camps for students of colleges.

In keeping with the trend of the recent worldwide phenomenon of entrepreneurship development through area approach, IIE initiated cluster development efforts to develop the languishing small and traditional industrial sector in the North Eastern Region with financial linkage.

IIE has been mandated the role of technical agency for 14 clusters in khadi, village industry and coir sector. IIE has conducted a series of seminars/workshops covering various aspects of the implementation of the programme. In addition, IIE has also facilitated linkage with various professional and support institutions for planned capacity building activities for different clusters. IIE has assisted the implementing agencies in product development both through design development and technology infusion by providing linkages with designers, technologists and institutions like weavers service centres etc. For market promotion, IIE has assisted the different clusters through initiatives like development of e-portal, conducting and facilitating buyer-seller meets, facilitating exhibition participation, providing linkages with marketing experts and retail houses etc.

## 16.2 Development and Training Institutes for Micro, Small and Medium Enterprises (MSMEs)

**16.2.1 National Institute for Micro, Small and Medium Enterprises (NI-MSME), Hyderabad:** See section 16.1.1 of this chapter.

**16.2.2 Other Development Institutes for MSMEs:**

**A. MSME Development Institutes (MSME-DIs):** The network of 30 MSME-DIs and 28 Branch MSME-DIs, set up in the State capitals and other industrial cities all over the country, mainly performs the following functions:

1. Organizing industrial motivation campaign/entrepreneurship, management and skill development programmes.
2. Assistance/consultancy to prospective and existing entrepreneurs.
3. Preparing state and district industrial potential survey reports.
4. Preparation/updation of project profiles of products/industries suitable and feasible in the MSMEs sector.
5. Conducting energy conservation, pollution control, quality control and upgradation.
6. Assisting ancillary development.
7. Making available common facility services in workshops/laboratories.
8. Preparation of directory of specific industries.
9. Market surveys.
10. Coordination with DICs and linkages with State Government functionaries.

11. Promotion and handholding of micro and small enterprises under Rajiv Gandhi Udyami Mitra Yojana (RGUMY).

**B. MSME Tool Rooms (MSME-TRs):** In present day fast-paced global business scenario, technology has become more vital than ever before. With a view to foster the growth of MSMEs, Government has set up tool rooms and training centres. These tool rooms provide valuable service to the Indian industry by way of precision tooling and providing well-trained craftsmen in the area of tool and die making. These tool rooms are highly proficient in mould and die making technology and promote precision and quality in the development and manufacture of sophisticated moulds, dies and tools. The tool room and training centres also offer various training programmes to meet the wide spectrum of technical manpower required in the manufacturing sector. The training programmes are designed with optimum blend of theory and practice giving the trainees exposure on actual jobs and hands on working experience. The tool rooms have also developed special training programmes to meet the requirements at international level, which are attended by participants from all over the globe.

The 10 MSME-TRs, set up under the Indo-German and Indo-Danish collaborations, assist MSMEs in technical upgradation and provide good quality tooling through designing and producing tools, moulds, jigs and fixtures, components etc. These tool rooms also provide technical training and consultancy in the area of tool and die making. The names and locations of different tool rooms are as under:

1. MSME-Tool Room (Central Tool Room), Ludhiana.
2. MSME-Tool Room (Indo-German Tool Room), Ahmedabad.
3. MSME-Tool Room (Indo-German Tool Room), Indore.
4. MSME-Tool Room (Indo-German Tool Room), Aurangabad.
5. MSME-Tool Room (Central Tool Room and Training Centre), Kolkata.
6. MSME-Tool Room (Central Tool Room and Training Centre), Bhubaneswar.

7. MSME-Tool Room (Indo-Danish Tool Room), Jamshedpur.
8. MSME-Tool Room (Central Institute of Hand Tools), Jalandhar.
9. MSME-Tool Room (Central Institute of Tool Design), Hyderabad.
10. MSME-Tool Room (Tool Room and Training Centre), Guwahati.

**C. MSME Technology Development Centres (MSME-TDCs):** These are product-specific centres for addressing product-specific problems and rendering technical services, developing and upgrading technologies and manpower development and training in respective product groups like foundry and forging, electronics, fragrance and flavour, sport shoes, electrical measuring instruments and glass.

Names and locations of different MSME-TDCs are as under:

1. Electronics Service and Training Centre (ESTC), Ramnagar.
2. Institute for Design of Electrical Measuring Instruments (IDEMI), Mumbai.
3. Fragrance and Flavour Development Centre (FFDC), Kannauj.
4. Centre for Development of Glass Industry (CDGI), Firozabad.
5. Process and Product Development Centre (PPDC), Agra.
6. Process-cum-Product Development Centre (PPDC), Meerut.

The main objective of MSME-TDCs is to develop human resources for meeting the requirements for transfer of technology in respective products fields. Some of them are also running training courses as per the requirements of the industry. The CDGI, Firozabad provides technical support to micro and small glass units through promoting installation of energy efficient glass melting furnaces, auxiliary furnaces, introduction of new types of glasses and their standardization, introduction of developed techniques for the decoration of glasswares etc.

**D. MSME Testing Centres (MSME-TCs):** These centres

located in Chennai, Delhi, Kolkata and Mumbai have facilities for quality upgradation, training/consultancy in testing, quality control, quality management, process quality control systems etc.

MSME-TCs provide testing and calibration facilities to industries in general and MSMEs in particular for raw materials, semi-finished and finished products, manufactured by them. The centres are equipped with the state-of-the-art indigenous and imported equipment in the field of chemical, mechanical, metallurgical and electrical engineering to undertake performance tests, type tests and acceptance tests of semi-finished, finished products etc. The centres also undertake calibration works for measuring instruments and equipment conforming to international standards. These centres are accredited by internationally recognized National Accreditation Board of Testing and Calibration Laboratories (NABL) certification as per ISO (17025).

**E. MSME Testing Stations (MSME-TSs):** In order to provide testing facilities in the area with cluster of industries and some strategic areas, MSME-TSs have been set up in Jaipur, Bhopal, Kolhapur, Hyderabad, Bangalore, Puducherry and Ettumanur. These testing stations extend facilities for testing of various products, viz. chemicals, dye-stuffs, lamps, rubber products, castings and forgings, paints and varnishes, domestic electrical appliances, general engineering etc.

These testing stations in fact act as extensions of MSME-TCs thereby serving the needs of the industries situated in far-flung areas.

**F. MSME Technology Development Centres (Central Footwear Training Institutes) (MSME-TDCs-CFTI):** These centres located in Agra and Chennai are engaged in developing designs and development of footwear and also providing training for skill development to footwear industry.

The basic objective of these centres is to develop human resources for footwear and allied industries through various training programmes on footwear technology and allied services. These centres conduct long-term, short-term and part-time training courses on different subjects of footwear technology. Besides, they provide technical support services to the user industry through making their facilities available to them. They also provide services for development of new products and patterns as per given sample or concept.

In short, the institutional and legal framework for promotion and development of micro, small and medium enterprises (MSMEs) sector of India is spread both at the national and state level. The primary responsibility for the development of MSMEs lies with the State Governments. Government of India supplements their efforts through a range of initiatives. The employment-intensive MSMEs sector has suffered extensively due to plethora of laws, rules and regulations that have accumulated during the years of control regime. Ensuring compliance with so many regulations coupled with *Inspector Raj* has stifled growth of the sector considerably.

The district industries centres under State Governments and MSME Development Institutes of Ministry of MSMEs provide facilitation to the new and existing entrepreneurs in developing their enterprises. With the implementation of Micro, Small and Medium Enterprises Development (MSMED) Act, 2006, two new sectors were classified in the country, i.e. medium sector and service sector, which required special attention for promotion and growth as these sectors were identified for the first time in any statute.

Introduction of filing of entrepreneurs memorandum under the MSMED Act was an important initiative towards liberalisation of the MSMEs sector. This provision liberated the entrepreneurs from the hurdles of registration of enterprises required under previous policy regime, for availing institutional finance and infrastructural support.

Provision of the delayed payment under the MSMED Act was another facilitator for ensuring regular cash flow to micro and small enterprises against the supplies made. Micro and small enterprises facilitation councils (MSEFCs) stipulated under the Act to be set up at the State level were foreseen as facilitators to the MSEs. However, most of these MSEFCs are not operating efficiently. In fact, in some states they are yet to be constituted.

### 16.3 Rajiv Gandhi Udyami Mitra Yojana (RGUMY)

World over, micro and small enterprises (MSEs) are recognized as an important/constituent of the national economies, contributing significantly to employment expansion and poverty alleviation. Recognizing the importance of micro and small enterprises, which constitute an important segment of Indian economy in terms of their contribution to country's industrial production, exports, employment and creation of entrepreneurial base, the Central and State Governments have been implementing several schemes and programmes for promotion and development of these enterprises.

The small scale industries in India, including the tiny or micro industries and service/business entities, collectively referred as micro and small enterprises (MSEs), have a long history of promoting inclusive, spatially widespread and employment-oriented economic growth. In terms of employment generation, this segment is next only to agriculture.

Entrepreneurship development and training is one of the key elements for development and promotion of micro and small enterprises, particularly, the first generation entrepreneurs. Entrepreneurship development programmes (EDPs) of various durations are being organized on regular basis by a number of organizations e.g. national and state level entrepreneurship development institutes (EDIs), micro, small and medium enterprises development institutes (MSMEDIs) [earlier known as small industries service institutes (SISIs)], national and state level industrial development corporations, banks and other training institutions/agencies in private and public sector etc., to create new entrepreneurs by cultivating their latent qualities of entrepreneurship and enlightening them on various aspects necessary for setting up micro and small enterprises. Besides, various industrial training institutes (ITIs), other private training institutions are also organizing vocational training (VT) programmes, skill development programmes (SDPs) and entrepreneurship-cum-skill development programmes (ESDPs).

However, there are still wide spread variations in the success rate, in terms of actual setting up and successful running of enterprises, by the EDP/SDP/ESDP trained entrepreneurs. It has been observed that entrepreneurs particularly new entrepreneurs, generally face difficulties in availing full benefits under available schemes of the Governments/financial institutions, completing and complying with various formalities and legal requirements under various laws/regulations, in selection of appropriate technology, tie-up with buyers and sellers etc. In order to bridge the gap between the aspirations of the potential entrepreneurs and the ground realties, there is a need to support and nurture the potential first generation as well as existing entrepreneurs by giving them handholding support, particularly during the initial stages of setting up and managing their enterprises.

In order to improve the success rate of the entrepreneurship development programme (EDP) trainees in the establishment of new enterprises, the Ministry of MSMEs launched a scheme, namely *Rajiv Gandhi Udyami Mitra Yojana* (a scheme for Promotion and Handholding of Micro and Small Enterprises). The main objective of this scheme is to provide handholding support to first generation entrepreneurs through designated lead agencies, i.e. *Udyami Mitras*. Under this scheme, the *Udyami Mitras* are providing guidance and assistance to the potential entrepreneurs registered with them in: (a) preparation of project reports, (b) arrangement of finance, (c) selection of technology, (d) marketing tie-ups with buyers, (e) installation of plant and machinery, and (f) obtaining various approvals, clearances etc. For providing this handholding assistance to the new entrepreneurs, the *Udyami Mitras* are paid handholding charges under the scheme, including nominal contribution of the concerned entrepreneur. However, the beneficiaries belonging to SCs, STs, physically handicapped and women are subsidized under the scheme for availing the handholding support from *Udyami Mitra*.

**16.3.1 Objectives of RGUMY:** These are as under:

1. To provide handholding support and assistance to the potential first generation entrepreneurs, who have already successfully completed or undergoing entrepreneurship development training programme (EDP)/skill development training programme (SDP)/entrepreneurship-cum-skill development training programme (ESDP)/vocation training programmes (VT), through the selected lead agencies i.e. *Udyami Mitras*, in the establishment and management of the new enterprise, in dealing with various procedural and legal hurdles and in completion of various formalities required for setting up and running of the enterprise.
2. To provide information, support, guidance and assistance to first generation entrepreneurs and other existing entrepreneurs through *Udyami Helpline* (a call centre for MSMEs), to guide them regarding various promotional schemes of the Government, procedural formalities required for setting up and running of the enterprise and help them in accessing bank credit etc.

**16.3.2 Udyami Mitras:**

**A. Eligibility:** Under RGUMY, financial assistance would be provided to the selected lead agencies, i.e. *Udyami Mitras* for rendering assistance and handholding support to the potential first generation entrepreneurs. Following agencies/organizations can be appointed as the lead agency, i.e. *Udyami Mitra*:

1. Existing national level entrepreneurship development institutions (EDIs).
2. Micro, small and medium enterprises development institutes (MSMEDIs)/branch MSMEDIs.
3. Central/State Government public sector enterprises (PSEs) involved in promotion and development of MSEs e.g. National Small Industries Corporation (NSIC) and State Industrial Development Corporations etc.

4. Selected State level EDIs and entrepreneurship development centres (EDCs) in public or private sector.
5. Khadi and Village Industries Commission (KVIC).
6. Special purpose vehicles (SPVs) set up for cluster development involved in entrepreneurship development.
7. Capable associations of MSEs/SSIs.
8. Other organizations/training institutions/NGOs etc. involved in entrepreneurship development/skill development.

**B. Role and Responsibilities of *Udyami Mitras*:** The selected lead agencies i.e. *Udyami Mitras* would be expected to render assistance and handholding support for following services:

1. Networking, coordinating and follow up with various Government departments, agencies, organizations and regulatory agencies on the one hand and with support agencies like banks/financial institutions, district industries centres (DICs), technology providers, infrastructure providers on the other hand, to help the first generation entrepreneurs in setting up their enterprise. *Udyami Mitras* are expected to help the first generation entrepreneurs in the following manner:

- Identification of suitable project/product/enterprise and preparation of bankable project report for the same.
- Assistance and support in establishment of work shed/office.
- Sanction of power load/connection.
- Selection of appropriate technology and installation of plant and machinery and office equipment etc.
- Obtaining various registrations, licenses, clearances and no objection certificates (NOCs).
- Allotment of income tax permanent account number (PAN) and service tax/sales tax/VAT registration etc.
- Sanction of working capital loan from the banks.
- Arranging tie up with raw material suppliers.
- Preparation and implementation of marketing strategy for the product/service and market development.
- Creation of web page and email identity.

2. Once the enterprise has been successfully set up, the *Udyami Mitras* would also monitor and follow up on the functioning of the enterprise for a further period of minimum 6 months and provide help in overcoming various managerial, financial and operational problems.

## 16.4 Other Schemes for Entrepreneurship Development

**16.4.1 Self-Employment and Talent Utilisation (SETU):** The National Policy for Skill Development and Entrepreneurs envisaged fostering entrepreneurship and grassroots innovation by providing support in terms of fiscal incentives, creation of grassroots technology innovation hubs, legal support and market linkages. The Government has established a mechanism to be known as SETU under NITI Aayog to support all aspects of start-up businesses and other self-employment activities, particularly in technology-driven areas.

As stated in the Budget Speech of the Finance Minister, 2015-16, SETU is to be a Techno-Financial, Incubation and Facilitation Programme to support all aspects of start-up businesses and other self-employment activities, particularly in technology-driven areas. Initially, a sum of ₹ 1,000 crore was set aside for the purpose

NITI Aayog constituted an Expert Committee on Innovation and Entrepreneurship (Chairman: Tarun Khanna) in April 2015 for working out the detailed contours of the Atal Innovation Mission (AIM) and SETU to achieve the stated objectives. The Committee submitted its report in August 2015.

**16.4.2 India Aspiration Fund (IAF):** In August 2015, Government launched IAF to be set up as a fund of funds under the Small Industries Development Bank of India (SIDBI) in order to boost the start-up ecosystem in the country. An initial corpus of ₹ 400 crore has been already allocated to various venture funds under it. The objective of the IAF is to catalyse tens of thousands of crores of equity investment into start-ups and MSMEs creating employment of lakhs of persons, mostly educated youth, over the next four to five years.

The fund has committed up to ₹ 60 crore in IvyCap Ventures, up to ₹ 30 crore for Blume Ventures and up to ₹ 20 crore for Carpediem Capital Partners.

India is witnessing a start-up revolution and to harness the potential of India's innovators and entrepreneurs a vibrant financial ecosystem is essential. IAF will play a vital role in this financial ecosystem.

This is a well-structured fund and since it is built on sectoral allocation, it will provide investment to start-ups in sectors which are not hot today for venture funds but will become hot in future.

**16.4.3 SIDBI Make in India Loan for Small Enterprises (SMILE):** SMILE was launched in August 2015. The objective of SMILE scheme is to provide soft loans in the nature of quasi-equity and term loans on relatively soft terms to MSMEs. The loan scheme's focus will be on 25 sectors under Government's Make in India programme with emphasis on financing smaller enterprises within the MSME sector.

The Department of Electronics and Information Technology is implementing a scheme entitled 'Technology Incubation and Development of Entrepreneurs' (TIDE) under which 147 start-ups have been supported at 25 TIDE centres established in premier institutes like IITs, NITs, IIMs etc.

**Endnotes**

1. National Institute for Entrepreneurship and Small Business Development (NIESBUD) was transferred to Ministry of Skill Development and Entrepreneurship (MSDE) on May 2, 2015.
2. Indian Institute of Entrepreneurship (IIE), Guwahati was transferred to Ministry of Skill Development and Entrepreneurship (MSDE) on May 2, 2015.

# Bibliography

# Bibliography

Anand Singh, K. and Krishna, K.V.S.M. (1994), "Agricultural Entrepreneurship: The Concept and Evidence", *Journal of Entrepreneurs*, Vol. 3, No. 1, March.

Arora, R. and Sood, S.K. (2007), "Fundamentals of Entrepreneurship and Small Business", in Baporikar, N. (ed.), 'Entrepreneurship Development and Project Management', Himalaya Publication House, New Delhi.

Arvinda, Ch. (2001), "Women Entrepreneurs: An Exploratory Study", Public Opinion Survey, Indian Institute of Public Opinion, New Delhi.

Beena, C. and Sushma, B. (2003), "Women Entrepreneurs Managing Petty Business: A Study from Motivational Perspective", *Southern Economist*, Vol. 42, May.

Chakrabarti, M. (2004), "Value Education: Changing Perspectives", Kanishka Publishers, New Delhi.

Chandra Lekha, R.S. (1995), "Value Education for College Students", *University News*, Association of Indian Universities, New Delhi.

Chandra, Kohil Shanta (1991), "Development of Women Entrepreneurship in India", Mittal Publications, New Delhi.

Choudhury, P.K., Shashi, Baijal and Asokan, M. (1997), "Bank and Women Enterprise Development: A Comparison of Approaches in India and UK", SEDME, XXIV, National Institute of Micro, Small and Medium Enterprises.

Deshpande, M.U. (1984), "Entrepreneurship of Small-scale Industries", Deep and Deep Publications, New Delhi.

Dhameja, S.K., Bhatia, B.S. and Saini, J.S. (2000), "Women Entrepreneurs: Their Perceptions about Business Opportunities and Attitudes towards Entrepreneurial Support Agencies", SEDME, 27/4, National Institute of Micro, Small and Medium Enterprises.

Dreze, J., and A. Sen (1996), "India: Economic Development and Social Opportunity", Oxford University Press, New Delhi.

Dubhashi, P.R. (1994), "Indian System of Higher Education", *University News*, February.

Government of India, Ministry of Finance, "Economic Survey", (various years).

—Planning Commission, "Report of the Working Group on Skill Development and Vocational Training", 2006.

Heckman, J.J. (2008), "Schools, Skills, and Synapses", *Economic Inquiry,* 46(3), pp. 289-324.

Kirve and Kanitkar (1993), "Entrepreneurship at the Grassroots: Developing the Income Generating Capabilities of Rural Women", *Journal of Entrepreneurship*, Vol. 2, No. 1, July.

Kulkarni, Manu N. (1996), "Evolving a Women's Policy", *Economic and Political Weekly*, Vol. 31, No. 12, March 23.

Leo, Paul Dona (1993), "Environment for Entrepreneurship: A Model of Public Policy and Economic Development", *The Journal of Entrepreneur*, Vol. 2, No. 1, September.

Mahanty, Sangram Keshari (2005), "Fundamentals of Entrepreneurship", Prentice Hall of India, New Delhi.

Panandikar, Surekha (1985), "Women Entrepreneurs: Problems and Potentials", *Economic Times*, December 26.

Pillai, Jaya Kothai (1995), "Women and Empowerment", Gyan Publishing House, New Delhi.

Rani, M. (1986), "Potential Women Entrepreneurs: A Study", SEDME, 13(3), National Institute of Micro, Small and Medium Enterprises.

Rao, Harinarayana (1991), "Promotion of Women Entrepreneurship", SEDME, Vol. 18, No. 2, National Institute of Micro, Small and Medium Enterprises, March.

Rao, N. (1991), "Counselling and Guidance", Tata McGraw Hill, New Delhi.

Sahoo, P.K. and Kumar, A. (2006), "Study of Networking of

Institutions in Promoting Quality of Students Support Services in Open Universities", *The UPRTOU Journal of Research and ODL Studies*, Vol. I.

Scarpetta, S., Pages, C. and Pierre, G. (2008), "Job Creation in Latin America and the Caribbean", The World Bank, Washington D.C.

Sonobe, T., Mano, Y., Akoten, J. and Otsuka, K. (2010), "Assessing the Impact of Management Skill Training in Ghana and Kenya", The World Bank, Washington D.C.

Suresh Reddy, J. (2004), "Entrepreneurship: Concept and Development", *Third Concept*, Vol. 17, June-August.

Tilak, J.B.G. (2002), "Vocational Education and Training in Asia", in John P. Keeves (ed.), 'The Handbook on Educational Research in the Asia Pacific Region', Kluwer Academic Publishers, Watanabe.

Tulus, Tambunan (2009), "Women Entrepreneurship in Asian Developing Countries: Their Development and Main Constraints", *Journal of Development and Agricultural Economics,* Vol. 1, No. 2, May.

Udaykumar, M.A. (2002), "Entrepreneurship Development Programmes (EDPs) and the Development of Entrepreneurs: A Study", *Small Enterprise Development Management Extension*, Vol. 29, No. 4, April.

Udaykumar, M.A. and Sreehdhara, T.N (2002), "Entrepreneurship Development Programmes: An Analysis", *Southern Economist*, Vol. 54, May.

UNESCO (1998), "World Education Report: Teachers and Teaching in a Changing World", UNESCO, Paris.

Vasanthakumari, G. (2012), "Economic Empowerment of Women through Micro Enterprises in India with Special Reference to Promotional Agencies", *International Journal of Multidisciplinary Research*, Vol. 2, No. 1, January.

Vijayan, P. and Geetha, T. (2006), "Integrated and Inclusive Education", Kanishka Publications, New Delhi.

Vinze, Megha Dubhashi (1987), "Women Entrepreneurs in

India: A Socio-economic Study of Delhi", Mittal Publications, New Delhi.

Walther, R. and Filipiak, E. (2007), "Vocational Training for the Informal Sector", Agence Francaise de Development, Fluitman.

World Bank (1995), "Investing in Young Children", World Bank Discussion Paper 275, The World Bank, Washington D.C.

World Bank (2003), "Lifelong Learning in the Global Knowledge Economy: Challenges for Developing Countries", The World Bank, Washington D.C.

***Websites***

Ministry of Skill Development and Entrepreneurship
Ministry of Human Resource Development
Ministry of Labour and Employment
Ministry of Micro, Small and Medium Enterprises
Ministry of Social Justice and Empowerment

# Index

# Index